To
a

Fly, Raven, Fly!

Katherine Kerestman
"Creepy Cat"

CREEPY CAT'S MACABRE TRAVELS

Creepy Cat's Macabre Travels
Copyright © 2020
Katherine Kerestman

ISBN: 978-1-952474-24-8

Cover concept and design by Jonathan Grisham for Grisham Designs.

Published by WordCrafts Press
Cody, Wyoming 82414
www.wordcrafts.net

CREEPY CAT'S MACABRE TRAVELS

Prowling Around Haunted Towers, Crumbling Castles, and Ghoulish Graveyards

KATHERINE KERESTMAN

WordCrafts

Contents

Creepy Cat cordially invites her reader to accompany her as she revisits a selection of splendidly weird destinations. What these places have in common is an association with the Macabre. Along the way, we will undoubtedly uncover some additional, even curious, facets of an array of cultures, histories, and philosophies. Merely for convenience, this book is organized geographically; there are sections on Europe, the United States, Mexico, and China.

Drawn from fiction, history, film and television, the stories that have inspired Creepy Cat's travels offer murky, cobwebbed windows into the human experience. Chilling tales of haunting, surreal, and inhuman entities that frighten us have been told by people of all times, and every place. It is the angst and insecurity which come with being human that these horror stories express. It turns out that, in the process of describing these forces and creatures (that which we are not), we are defining by negation our own humanity (that which we are).

The struggle to understand our nature and our relation to—well, to everything else—is the lot of humans everywhere. All of us share in this struggle to find meaning in a mysterious, indifferent universe. As Creepy Cat travels, albeit usually purely for pleasure, as a humanist she cannot help putting two and two together and realizing that our common fears, aversions, and yearnings can some- times unite people—and can also drive them into opposing camps. These are the mysteries told by the story-weavers of macabre tales.

The result of Creepy Cat's travels to zombie graveyards and prehistoric settlements is an appreciation of the insecurity of the human being. Creepy Cat feels compassion for the proud, preening, cruel, horrified, spooked, and amazed human creature that is at heart afraid and alone in a scary universe, and who examines this witches' brew of emotions through horror stories and macabre tales in every place and time.

The tones of the articles vary accordingly, as the full range of human nature is considered through a dark mirror. Creepy Cat requests that you hold onto your seat.

CREEPY CAT
PUTS HER BEST PAW FOREWORD

PART I
WHEREIN CREEPY CAT PUTS FORTH HER PHILOSOPHY OF TRAVEL

A reader of Creepy Cat's article entitled *Salem Past and Present Intermixt* commented that it would be better had she not joined history, travel, tourism, and personal commentary in a single travel narrative. Were philosophy, history, sightseeing, literature, science, industry, culture, and government each relegated to separate compartments—well, Creepy Cat would be a different breed of cat, and this book an almanac. For Creepy Cat, roaming the streets and back alleys of the world means stepping into other paw prints, other times and places. Creepy Cat enjoys periodically shedding one of her lives, her fur, and her perspective, to try on different lives. Creepy Cat sometimes prepares for her expeditions by prowling around the history, cuisine, and culture of her destination. For her, every step of the way is anthropology and each border crossing a link with the greater-than-me, a glimpse of the collective.

Creepy Cat reflects that where she places her paw now countless feet have padded—bare feet, Roman-sandaled feet, courtly curled-over-toe-shoed feet, or sneakered feet—each one of them bearing a head bursting with ideas. Creepy Cat knows that each of us is the cool cat she is because of the convictions, passions, discoveries and dreams of cats who have stood before where we stand now and who have woven their skeins of yarn into a cat's cradle of networks. With each journey Creepy Cat can experience anew the wondrous permutations of the fabric we are weaving together in the common loom of life. Thus, Creepy Cat recalibrates her perspectives when she travels: she reflects that her experiences are not discrete, not solitary, but part of a communal endeavor wherein together we weave the tapestry of existence.

Nonetheless, Creepy Cat is not a staid old cat that knocks about the dust balls on old books. She likes, above all, to play, to knock about a ball of yarn and unravel the threads. As she roams the world seeing the sights, browsing boutiques, and eating new foods, Creepy Cat gains insight and learns more about herself and the world without even trying. Usually she travels to places she thinks are *the cat's meow*, places she has learned of in books. (It can be risky to give her a book because, once this cat's curiosity is aroused, she will want to see a place for herself.)

PART II
CREEPY CAT OFFERS SUGGESTIONS FOR PLANNING EXCURSIONS

Creepy Cat wishes to confess that she does not travel lightly and prefers to unpack only once, and therefore chooses a centrally located hotel in the region she is exploring. She begins by studying a map from which to select a center of operations which is where her hotel should be located, and then she looks for interesting experiences that are near enough to the center for day trips from her hotel. Creepy Cat recommends the traveler create her list of all the landmarks she would like to see—as well as out-of-the-way mouse holes that arouse her curiosity—and then calculate how many days she should stay to realize her plan. Creepy Cat adds one or two days more for the unexpected enjoyments she will discover after she has arrived. At this point, it is time to reserve the hotel room.

Once Creepy Cat has chosen a hotel, she has obtained a concierge, a local person with a great deal of logistics savvy to share; from the concierge she can get information from someone on the ground before leaving home—about train schedules, obtaining tickets for theater, dining, guided bus tours departing from the hotel, and museum hours. (For instance, someone who lives in that city can tell her all the museums are closed on Monday, but that Monday is a good day for cathedral tours.) Creepy Cat feels comfortable traipsing around Europe and North America. Time after time, she has found the people cordial and free with information for the American tourist cat. It is generally easy to strike up a conversation in a restaurant or at a train station, and the foreign people she has spoken with generally ask as many questions about America as she asks them about their countries.

There have been a few exceptions to the rule of Creepy Cat's usual independent approach to traveling. The first time she traveled to Paris she voyaged via a Seine River cruise—it was her first expedition to Europe. Overall, it was a satisfying experience, for she had chosen a vessel that sailed primarily overnight so that she might be on land all day. Despite the excellence of the itinerary, though, she felt confined, for she prefers to prowl all day long and see everything she can; typically, she leaves the hotel at sunrise and returns late at night. She departed the cruise boat a day early and headed for Paris, because she needed to strike out on her own. (Creepy Cat reminds the Reader that cats are independent creatures.) Another time, she chose to travel to China with an escorted tour, for China is a communist country and she felt safer in a group on that particular trip; besides, fewer Chinese than Europeans speak English. (It was a grand experience—she saw Beijing, Chongqing, Xian, and Shanghai, and found the Chinese people friendly and as curious about her as she was about them.)

Creepy Cat has found it advantageous to hire a private driver on occasion. From Sorrento, Italy, for instance, there was no convenient way to go to the top of Mt. Vesuvius and Pompeii, so she made use of a driver for those excursions. A *History Channel* program about *Poenari Castle* at the top of a mountain in the Carpathians of Transylvania stirred her to visit Transylvania; outside of Bucharest, however, transportation in Romania is a bit more difficult to manage than it is in more western European countries, because Romania is largely rural and the Dracula sites she went to visit are dispersed over a large area. Being a free spirit and knowing from her ample reading about Dracula and Vlad the Impaler precisely what places she wished to see in Transylvania, Creepy Cat hired a private guide (which was not as costly as she would have imagined) and she created her own itinerary. The trip turned out well: the local guides showed her even more ancient sites than she had been aware of (sites not related to Dracula) and they helped her to fill out her exploration of Romania.

PART III
CREEPY CAT GETS LOST

Once or twice Creepy Cat could not find her way. From Cologne to Bonn she had taken a Rhine River cruise, and after having visited Beethoven's birthplace and the Old Town of Bonn, Creepy Cat took a cab to a museum in another part of the city. After her taxi had left her and driven away, she found that the museum was closed and no other taxis were to be found in the vicinity; neither could Creepy Cat discover any English-speaking person who was able to assist her to find her way back to the Bonn train station (and from there back to Cologne and then Brussels). She wandered around Bonn until she lighted upon a United Nations building. As she approached it a disembodied voice called to her to come no closer unless she had a United Nations escort. Creepy Cat stayed put and asked for directions, which the disembodied voice was not able to provide her. At length Creepy Cat came to a young woman who turned out to be a student at the university; on her way to the subway, she kindly took Creepy Cat with her and helped her to find her way back.

In Waterloo Creepy Cat found an opportunity to make the acquaintance of a local cat by requiring assistance once more.

Creepy Cat had gone by rail from Brussels to Waterloo to see the *Lion's Mound* and Battle of Waterloo museums. It turned out that Waterloo is a smaller town and no one who spoke English was in the train station when Creepy Cat arrived there, resulting in a little problem arranging a taxi to the places she had come to see. Creepy Cat was pleased to see a woman letting several young misses out of her car—girls laden with quantities of home-baked pastries. Creepy Cat inquired of the Belgian lady whether the girls were Girl Scouts, and it turned out they were the Belgian equivalent of Girl Scouts, whereupon Creepy Cat purchased some of their delicious treats and the lady gave her a lift to the *Lion's Mound* in her own car. Although Creepy Cat prides herself on her logistical abilities, she has found that occasionally losing one's way or needing assistance can be a good way to meet people while abroad.

PART IU
CREEPY CAT PUTS HER BEST PAW FORWARD

Creepy Cat tries to always keep in mind that she is an ambassadress when she is abroad, and that people who live in other countries may judge all American cats by her. Creepy Cat realizes that when she is a traveler she is a guest in someone else's home, and that she has no territorial claims or rights outside of her own home. She makes an effort to be polite and to let people know that she is obliged for their hospitality. Not knowing all the subtle customs of every place, Creepy Cat probably makes some fauxpaws without even realizing it, and she appreciates when her hosts understand that she means no offense. Creepy Cat tries to let foreign cats know she is appreciative also that they speak English in addition to their own native tongues.

It is a fortunate thing that cats have nine lives, because Creepy Cat wishes to see every place, and it is a pretty big world in which to pussyfoot around in only a single lifetime. Creepy Cat wishes her Reader *Happy Travels*, whether from indulging his own wanderlust or from stowing away on Creepy Cat's adventures.

Old World Macabre

H onfleur, a coastal town on the English Channel, on the northern coast of France, is the first city I visited on my maiden voyage to Europe. Honfleur is a medieval town of tightly packed buildings, most of them four stories tall, built around a large stone-paved square. Restaurants and shops operate out of the first floors of the medieval buildings, and sailboats dock at the wharf on the other side of the square. Constricted and snaking stone-paved medieval streets branch off from the square. My first impression of Europe on the inaugural day of my maiden journey was the closeness of medieval towns, where ancient structures are not museums, but are still functioning workplaces, homes, churches, and government buildings. Houses' front doors open right onto the sidewalks of the narrow streets; more than one door opened as I walked past it. Dwellers in medieval towns must have a different sense of personal space, a shorter comfort zone than Americans. Tiny cars and scooters are needed to navigate the narrow old streets. I spent the day enjoying French cuisine in the cafes and patisseries and splendid shopping in the charming boutiques (clearly not chain restaurants and department stores), where sales staff addressed me as "Madame" and paid me personal attention. From Honfleur I would be traveling a week on the River Seine to Paris, where I would stay another week. The river boat on which I was cruising would be sailing mostly at night, so that passengers could spend the days on land.

On my second day in France I experienced my first *ruined abbey* at Jumieges, and I have never been the same since. I had, of course, already a well-developed Gothic sensibility, derived from a lifetime of reading *Dracula* and the novels of Ann Radcliffe, Sir Walter Scott, Horace Walpole, and the Brontes (in addition, I had been raised on *Dark Shadows*, a daily after-school gothic supplement to my education). Yet, the multi-dimensional experience of walking at Jumieges on a chill, darkened cloudy October day, of being *in France*, of being hemmed in by crumbling walls, is not reproducible in words or film. There is mystery in a crumbling abbey. Walking on grass where stone floors used to be and through arches which no longer support any structure, you first question, "What happened?" Then you wonder about who was there and when. I looked at the stones and touched them and thought about who put them together, drawing upon my limited knowledge of medieval cathedral-building. There are inscriptions and pictures in the walls to decipher. I wondered, what this room was for, and that, and where did this corridor lead? I wanted to know what used to be down those steps. There are places where bright white light comes through the glass-less windows and other spaces commandeered by black shadows. When I left Jumieges I saw that modern development had cropped up all about the ancient structure. Past and present are not as separate in Europe as in America, where ancient structures are scarce, and it is not that difficult to imagine that the spirits of the dead still inhabit those shadows.

The river boat passed by Normandy's thatched houses, on the roofs of which grew living vegetation; and it passed lovely chateaux with towers wearing pointed roofs (those large houses have many little roofs instead of one great one) surrounded by gardens. We stopped at Trouville, where Gigi cavorted on the beach with Gaston, and in my heart, I sang *The Night They Invented Champagne*. I walked the boardwalk, empty now because the summer was gone. I preferred it that way, the better to confront the color-blocked view of the blue sky on top merged with the water of the English Channel, the straight line of the horizon separating it from the wide swath of brown sand on bottom. Behind me were nineteenth-century beach resort buildings of incredible, dignified *fin de siècle* beauty. I spent a few coins in the slot machines at the *Casino Barrierre de Trouville*.

Our next destination was Rouen, another medieval town, with my first visit to a living medieval cathedral—and it had all the anticipated gothic detailing, arched stained-glass windows, and gargoyles I had looked forward to. The Cathedral of Notre Dame de Rouen is a cold white marble, very-high ceiling edifice, flying buttresses soaring above, the marble statuary below medieval and stiff. Brown wooden chairs are arranged for parishioners in the cavernous interior. The most fascinating aspect is a crypt mounted with a marble reliquary sculpture of Richard Couer de Leon that contains his heart. Empress Matilda of England is also buried here. For centuries, England and France fought wars over this region of Normandy, directly across the English Channel from England.

In Rouen is *Le Bucher*, the place of execution of Jean d'Arc. Joan of Arc (her English name) lived in France 1412–1430. The illiterate young peasant girl miraculously earned the confidence of the French king and army. She provided encouragement to King Charles VII, served as his confidential advisor and military counselor, and even led his army as a soldier. Her contribution to Charles's military and political successes was not insubstantial. Being a peasant, and a female, however, intriguing court and ecclesiastical factions accused her of witchcraft and brought her down. Her own contemporaries, the Catholic Church, and present-day people are divided on whether she was a saint acting upon instructions given her by God, or a delusional madwoman. Whatever her mental state, Joan suffered quite horribly during her inquisition and refused to recant her claims of divine direction, and she was burned alive at the stake. A large steel pole that has a cross on top marks where she died. She is *Saint* Jean d'Arc now, and a French national hero.

The river boat followed the Seine to Caudebec, a cathedral beautiful for its highly sculpted walls which give it a lace-covered appearance when viewed from a distance. We also stopped at Giverny, home to Monet, and walked about the house, gardens, and water lily pond. Then we came to Chateau Bizy, which made me melancholy, for it was the home of the Princess de Lamballe, whose decapitated head was waved on a pike to her friend Marie Antoinette, who was in prison during the Revolution. It is a graceful eighteenth-century building around a circular courtyard with reflecting pool and formal gardens.

The river boat continued down the Seine through locks, past verdant tree-covered hills, to Les Andelys, where I climbed the narrow streets up to the prominence on which Richard Couer de Leon had built the Chateau Gaillard in 1197, now in a ruined state. Here I learned that some of the castles and abbeys had been dismantled by subsequent generations to recycle the building materials for new projects, a sense of historical conservatism not having been developed yet, not until the late eighteenth century, about the time when gothic sensibility and the gothic novel came into existence. By this time I was certain that I preferred ruined castles to intact. From that cliff-top ruin I looked down upon the town I had walked through and the winding Seine below, knowing that The Lionheart could very well have stood upon this spot to look down at the river below. This is *exactly* what I wanted to do in Europe.

The last stop on the river cruise was Versailles, the culmination of French Baroque splendor. Louis XIV had converted the hunting lodge of his father, Louis XIII, into a glorious palace, which was further augmented in grandeur under Louis XV, and which became the quintessence of beauty in interior design under Marie Antoinette and Louis XVI. The palace of Versailles exhibits power and wealth as well as the other courts of Europe, but not with so heavy a hand. Versailles has its opulent gold, marble, and mirrors, but its delicacy—of its pastels, embroidery, filigree, crystal, tracery and ormolus—is what creates the unique magnificence of Versailles. After I had lingered as long as I could at Versailles, I departed the river cruise a day early and set out for Paris on my own.

I tried to experience every aspect of Paris. On the Left Bank I explored dozens of antique stores, where candlesticks sold for a hundred thousand dollars (they used to belong to a princess), and I purchased a vintage French Mattel Barbie catalog for my collection. I enjoyed the can-can performance at the *Moulin Rouge*. On the Eiffel Tower, high above Paris, I sipped champagne. I promenaded on the Champs Elysee to the Arc de Triomphe, illuminated at night. I visited Sainte Chapelle, that beautiful blue and gold church, with radiant stained-glass windows, and star-sparkling blue ceiling at the jointure of the flying gold buttresses, truly a breathtaking interior. I visited the Invalides, the old military hospital/museum and looked at the tomb of Napoleon, once the most powerful man on earth, now dust in an elaborate box. I saw Marie Antoinette's cell in the Concierge. I spent a day at the Louvre, where a year would be insufficient for a thorough study of the buildings and their contents. In honor of Gigi, I supped at *Maxim's*, and then relished the Art Noveau collection in the *Musee D'Orsay*. The hours passed too quickly at the *Hotel de Cluny*, a museum of medieval art which was constructed upon third century Roman baths. Here are the *Lady and the Unicorn* tapestries.

By now I was able to understand why eighteenth and nineteenth-century Americans and Europeans on a *Grand Tour of the Continent* found these medieval buildings and works of art remote, suspect, and a little frightening. Modernity had transformed western society by that time—the age of steam, mechanization, railroads, and electricity had changed people even without their realizing it, and when they visited crumbling gothic buildings they no longer recognized themselves in the Catholic structures which had once delineated every aspect of life and defined one's very self for nearly two millennia. Usurped by Progress and Reason, the past seemed sinister and strange. Post-Reformation, Age of Reason tourists concocted fantastic stories in their imaginations when gazing at a past with which they no longer felt a connection: hence the gothic novel with its crumbling castles, locked towers, sinister medieval monks, dark shadows, and ghostly apparitions.

Notre Dame de Paris is no longer there; burned down recently, the world is banding together to rebuild it. Erected between 1163 and 1330, it had been re-built in part in the past, a victim of war and time. It is situated on *L'ile de la Cite*, the island in the Seine forming the heart of Paris. Its façade was formed of two three-story square towers that flanked a center of two stories, with three arched portals onto the street; on the second story were two arched doorways, statues of Adam and Eve on the left and right, with a rose window in between them. A tracery gallery filled with medieval monsters, from gargoyles to chimeras and demons was between the second and third stories. Over that were the two bell towers. The vast candlelit marble interior glowed golden in the flickering lights, any recesses unlit very dark and mysterious.

I walked the tracery level taking pictures of Paris over the shoulders of gargoyles and ghouls, attempting to capture on film the carvings on the walls and columns as well. The Eiffel Tower was very small in the distance. Climbing the narrow, spiral stone steps to the bell tower, I saw on the walls illustrations from Victor Hugo's *The Hunchback of Notre Dame*. In 1831 Victor Hugo found inspiration in the creepy monsters adorning this ancient edifice, which had been erected before European society espoused the concept of the worth of each individual—a groundbreaking new idea of the Renaissance. Hugo lived among the medieval monsters that were crawling all over public buildings of Paris, immense medieval edifices representative of an outdated feudal world view. Hugo's *The Hunchback of Notre Dame* is a thrilling gothic tale of the travails of characters from despised and suspect castes—women, gypsies, and the handicapped —played out in front of the unfeeling Notre Dame Cathedral, the earthly home of God the Father. In *The Hunchback of Notre Dame* the ecclesiastical and political hierarchy are the monsters devouring a struggling humanity.

Monsters and demons in art, architecture, and literature provide a vocabulary for representing our cruelty to one another. Victor Hugo recognized the irony of the griffins affixed to Notre Dame, placed there to frighten people into submission, a sculptural warning of the peril of being cast into hell. Medieval ecclesiastical and political hierarchies were hardly functioning as shepherds watching over their flocks: people suffered horrendously, from dying of starvation and cold to being burned at the stake. For many, the Church was a heartless monster dealing out cruel punishment, and life on earth a hell, so that some people might wonder what penalty after death could be as bad as the life they were enduring then. *The Hunchback of Notre Dame* depicts a miserable life on earth lived in the shadow of the Notre Dame Cathedral, a huge and imposing structure whose gargoyles were meant to intimidate, rather than inspire.

Questing for Monsters in the Low Countries

A thing of beauty is a joy forever, especially if it is a dark and macabre beautiful thing. Thus, I felt that I had reached Nirvana when I discovered Hieronymus Bosch in an undergraduate art history class. One of the benefits of pursuing a degree in the liberal arts is that one can read scary stories and look at pictures of monsters and count that as an education. Hunting down the grotesques and gruesome depictions of hell that filled my art history textbook was one of the objects of my trip to Brussels.

I stayed in an old landmark Brussels hotel near the Bourse and availed myself of a EuroRail pass so that I could traipse about that part of the continent. Despite the ravages of religious war in the sixteenth-century time of the Reformation, the Low Countries remain rich in late Medieval and early humanistic art. It was a time of uneasy transition from gold-leafed icons to natural humanism. The social and religious tensions of the period produced a frightening and uncomfortable mood, a mood that informed the artistic representation of sin and damnation, the perfect atmosphere for the creation of hellish monstrosities.

Belgium has much more to recommend it, of course, than monsters, and so I spent a couple of days exploring that marvelous city in the heart of Europe. My hotel was near the great medieval square, *Grande Place*, which is demarcated with exquisite gold-trimmed Baroque buildings housing shops, cafes, and museums. The *Maison de Roi* City Museum showcases art and artifacts pertaining to Brussels history and culture, numerous painted and carved altarpieces, and a treasury of gold-leaf medieval art. After visiting the museum, I sampled Belgian artisan chocolates and purchased lace in the shops on the square, and sipped champagne in the *Galleries Royale St. Hubert* , a nineteenth-century arcade that provides a sensory-rich retail experience. Art Noveau motifs sprinkle the square, which is filled with people, many sitting on the ground enjoying time with friends in the outdoor space. At night, as well, the squares are filled with people eating and drinking, with music from portable boom boxes, for dancing. Brussels is a social place all through the night.

In Brussels I visited the *Belvue Museum* and the *Palais du Coudenberg*, a twelfth-century palace destroyed by fire in the eighteenth century. The rubble was buried and serves now as the foundation of the Royal Quarter. The *Coudenberg* is an active archaeological excavation site beneath the street. Above it, sidewalk cafes bustle and people are moving about the cobblestones of the Rue Royale. Below ground is the now-quiet former Rue Isabelle. Rue Isabelle is now a tunnel, having been covered over by the construction of the new street and buildings, and visitors walk the underground street and enter doorways and rooms that were once street-level. Royal accoutrements are in cases, having been rescued from the rubble: pottery, goblets, and hardware. The palace below ground is a time capsule.

The *Musee de Beaux Arts* is an exquisite repository of the fine arts, home to a comprehensive Art Noveau collection. The *Musee* is situated near the Brussels *Tomb of the Unknown Soldier*, the gothic *Notre Dame de Sablis*, and the *fin de siècle* architecture of the *Mons des Arts*. The area is a veritable outdoor museum of architecture and design. Who would suppose that monsters dwell amidst all this glory?

The *Musee de Beaux Arts* contains a rich collection of fifteenth-century Flemish art. Art flourished at that time, when the Low Countries were the hub of international trade, and mercantile wealth enabled patronage of the arts. The art was largely religious in nature, but it was moving from standardized medieval iconography to humanistic naturalism. Hieronymus Bosch's *Crucifixion with a Donor* is in this museum. In contrast to countless Crucifixion scenes painted in the Middle Ages, Bosch's work is notable for the newly emerging attention to realism. Whereas medieval art was often characterized by gold leaf backgrounds, Bosch's detailed contemporary city landscape forms the background of his religious scene.

Heaven and Hell provided frequent counterpoints in religious art. Earthly existence is depicted as a time of making choices. Bosch's scenes of heaven are surreally naturalistic, and his earth a place where people tend to excess in the good things God has provided. But his Hell gets the most interest: dark burning cities; people crawling in and out of eggs and fruit big as cathedrals; orgies juxtaposed with combat; clergy hybrids with fish and pigs. Bosch represents heaven as a magnificently psychedelic, mellow place, but viewers tend to be drawn to the bizarre and frenzied scenes of Hell. There is much speculation about the meaning of Bosch's symbolism, scholars trying to find a key to his code in alchemy, Tarot, secret religious organizations, the Bible, Freudian theory, and moral allegory. His work does not utilize standardized traditional Christian or Romantic symbolism: he created his own.

Pieter Bruegel painted a similar fantasia. In *Fall of the Rebel Angels*, St. Michael has dragonfly wings and a bloated frog floats upside down, its sliced-open belly spilling its eggs. Squiggly red sea creatures put their tentacles between human legs, and huge fish swallow up the angels. One angel in an armor mask is merged with an armadillo, another helmeted fellow has arms like spiders' legs and no feet or legs.

I explored other parts of Brussels on foot and saw a conical medieval tower wedged between twentieth-century buildings, the *Brussels Bell Tower* and the *Church of St. Catherine* among modern blocks of restaurants, stores, and office buildings. I headed toward modern Brussels, to the *European Parliament*, whose mission is to prevent European nations from ever attacking each other again, warning how close they had come to annihilating each other during the wars of the last century, when nationalism had overcome reason. I went to the *Atomium*; built for the 1958 World Fair, it is over three hundred feet high, a collection of glinting stainless steel spheres about sixty feet in diameter, connected by tubes which contain escalators and light shows and carry visitors from one sphere to the next. From the panoramic restaurant in the top sphere, the trees below look like broccoli: Belgium today has the same technological energy it had in the fifteenth century when it was an international commercial hub.

I spent one day going to Luxembourg City by train, through the Ardennes Forest, the very name of which conjures chills when recalling the savage battles that were fought there in the World Wars. After exploring medieval fortifications built into the hillside and crumbling ancient towers, I enjoyed lunch at a café, where I encountered a couple from Ohio who were in Luxembourg to visit a child at college there; from them I learned that I had just missed running into Duchess Kate by one day.

In Antwerp—on another excursion from Brussels by train—I was imbibing the atmosphere of the *Grotemarket*, where I sat in the wind at the table of a sidewalk café. The overcast sky threatened imminent rain. A very large open space, the *Grotemarket* is a stone-paved square bordered by medieval guild houses. As I sat at the table, a colorful band of musicians, clad in orange, red, and purple, with horns and tambourines and flags marched by, giving freely of their music. I asked the waiter what the occasion was—a festival?—and he answered that there was no occasion, that they just did that. I walked to the River Scheldt and came to a colossal bronze sculpture of the *Scheldt River Giant* of old legends. I toured the *Peter Paul Rubens House* and the *Museum Plantin-Moretus*, home of a sixteenth-century printer.

Monsters abound in Cologne, Germany (which I reached by rail from Brussels) in the *Wallraf-Richartz* medieval museum in the shadow of the Cologne Cathedral. In one memorable painting, St. Anthony is being torn apart by red dogs with dragon wings and long, taloned feet, a green stag with red rams' horns, and a tooth-some monkey; St. Anthony's face expresses horror and disbelief, his arms hanging limply, while monsters' jowls are in his armpits. After a night in Cologne, and a Rhine River cruise to Bonn the next morning, I returned to Brussels.

Thence to the canal-ed town of Ghent (on another rail excursion), where a winged dragon sits atop the *Belfort Tower*, chin up, tail-raised, sailing o'er a music-box mechanical bell system, reached by the tourist via a flight of narrow and winding medieval stairs. After a quick dip into the *Ghent Design Studio*, a modern textile and furnishings design establishment, I plunged back into the past, to see the *Ghent Altarpiece* at the *Sant Baafskathedraal*.

The *Sant Baafskathedraal* is a cathedral of green marble and chocolate wood, interspersed with numerous white marble reliquaries of reclining ecclesiastics and cherubs and Biblical characters. The *Ghent Altarpiece* is deserving of its reputation. The colors alone are dazzling—rich ruby and emerald jewel tones. The achievement of depth, the mixture of sacred and profane, the rendering of the human form, and its resemblance to the divine—the effect of the whole is so much greater than even the sum of these parts. The altarpiece is a combination of technological breakthroughs and the artistic vision of a genius who could combine love of God and love of man with paint on wood.

From the *Baafskathedraal* I walked to the *Het-Gravensteen*, a twelfth-century castle which has been restored. Flags fly in the sunshine from its crenelated towers. I wove my way through Ghent's medieval streets, appreciating the gargoyles on the tops of the public buildings and the creatures appearing to fly over the guild halls' spires on which they are perched. In the *Museum voor Schone Kunsten*, there is a Bosch painting of *Christ Carrying the Cross*, in which a weary Christ appears to wish it were done, as he is pulled and pushed through a tightly-packed crowd of vicious-looking people; some appear to be mourning, while others snarl and growl and bare their teeth, as monstrous as any fantastic creature in his scenes of Hell, madness and destruction as plain as day in their faces. We have met the demons, and they are us.

Bruges and Ghent are wonderful canal cities, with medieval buildings up to the water's edge, swans swimming among the canal boats, floral gardens bordering the waterways, and overhanging trees. In Bruges is the *Basilica of the Blood*, which houses a relic of Christ's blood. Its blue and purple stained glass, dark red ceilings and green walls, and gold ornamentation are evocative of Byzantine churches. The *Stadhui* is a fully restored medieval town hall, with a yellow and green parquet floor, sumptuous woodwork, murals above the wainscoting, and a buttressed ceiling. The *Historium* provides a three-dimensional interactive experience which places the visitor in the milieu of Renaissance Bruges. At the *Groeninge Museum*, I located Jan Van Eyck paintings I had loved since that long-ago art class: Mrs. Van Eyck in her Bruges lace headgear, ermine and velvet gown; and *The Madonna and Canon Van der Paele*.

Here also is Bosch's *Last Judgement*, a triptych with a fantastic heaven on the left. Heaven includes a white tower; a gelatinous, succulent floating fruit with all kinds of antennae or sprouts; a lawn like a golf course; and a pleasure boat in a lake bearing a naked couple kneeling together in reverent innocence. On the right is a burnt-out city, scorched and blackened landscape, red sky, and fire pouring from the roof of a building on the horizon. In the center panel Christ in a red robe floats in a blue orb, flanked by angels and saints. The earth below heaven is a charred battleground in the aftermath of Armageddon. Courtly ladies in pointed hats and veils congregate under a tent that is crowned with fantastic tiny nude figures dancing around a bagpipe—an image that pulls the viewer's eyes into the tent and into the painting. A naked man is in a great shoe. Other naked people are in saddlebags of sorts on a giant hybrid mouse-rabbit, the saddlebag on the far side is a bird cage containing people, and the one on the side nearest the viewer is a metal cup with rivets holding a naked tonsured monk and a nun wearing only a wimple kissing. One nude man lies prone astride

25

an oversized knife. A blindfolded head lies near a headless body that crawls around on its hands and knees as if it were seeking its head, a spear through its trunk. Hybrid forms of flora and fauna create a discordant, discomforting sensation, thoroughly creepy, but captivating, drawing one's gaze into the dazzling array of miniature absurdities in a large and chaotic worldview—and the astounded viewer must endeavor to create sense of the bizarre jumble.

One of the last cities on my itinerary was Lille, France, a short train ride from Brussels. A charming, old-world town with vast grand plazas and rows of Baroque architecture, it is home to many chocolatiers and patisseries. I dined at *Monsieur Jean's*, where I had a couscous and root vegetable dish with a presentation that was splendid enough to inspire a still-life painting. Wrought iron balconies in rows three stories high ornament the boulevards. The modern *Notre Dame Cathedral* in Lille has a façade of marble which is so translucent that through it the sun can shine into the church.

The *Palais des Beaux-Arts* surpassed all the other delights of this city. (Someday I am going to visit a museum and focus on nothing but the magnificent frames around the paintings.) A life-size white marble sculpture of a satyr embracing (or raping) a woman arrested my attention. From behind you can see his tail coming from the small of his back, and the bottoms of his hooves and his hairy thighs as he kneels to grapple the woman. Joan of Arc is another of my favorite sculptures there, a white marble rendering of her at the stake, standing atop kindling.

And there is a work by Dieric Bouts, a Bosch-like painter, with a horrid scene of the pit of Hell, naked bodies cast in among horny-headed red monsters with eyes for nipples and rodent-like mouths. Amphibious monkeys and oversized lizards lie in a heap with mankind. A razor-toothed fish has its jaws around a man's head. Black winged creatures in the sky carry more people and drop them into the pit.

Bosch's *Singers in an Egg* is also in the *Beaux Arts* at Lille. A chorale group emerging from a cracked egg sing. A man in red plays a

26

flute. A monk points to a hymnal. A barren tree branch rises from the egg, and a limp green snake hangs from the branch. A round house with a thatched roof sits upon one man's head, and a stork sits on the flutist's red cap. A winged monkey plays a woodwind. A donkey dressed as a courtier strums a lute. To the left a miniature conflagration rages. It is the world created by a madman.

When Western Civilization made the leap from the safe territory of a received God-centered world view of the Middle Ages into the uncharted psychological and metaphysical regions of the Renaissance and Reformation, there must have been doubts and reservations and fear. Whether it was a leap of faith, or a rejection of faith, at this juncture in history humankind was facing the terror of the unknown, and this is reflected in the dark monsters of northern Renaissance art.

As viewers, we feel guilty in the act of enjoying darkly fantastical and enigmatic panoramas of horror, of warped humanity and grotesque beasts. Why, we wonder, do we like this stuff, the Macabre, when we are neither monsters nor evil people? We do because we share some measure of the uncertainty expressed by the artists. It is the ability to say, "I know how you feel," to share the common human fear of being an animalcule adrift in the cosmos, that is communicated through works of horror and the macabre. It is ourselves that we view. We gaze at the human condition, through a dark mirror.

Seeking Dracula in his Lair

My hunt for Count Dracula began with a two-day visit to Bucharest, Romania; the *Hotel Berthelot* was to be my home for this part of my journey. A nondescript, but clean, hotel with all necessary amenities and a breakfast buffet of breads, fruit, and cold meat and cheese, it was a comfortable base. I sought my dinner (and a requisite trophy t-shirt) at the *Hard Rock Café*, a grey block building with modernistic details. There weren't too many customers, and I asked my server to take my picture. Five waiters immediately surrounded me, and another shot our group photo. I was wearing my *Hard Rock* Beijing shirt, and the staff were full of questions about America and China. I always feel at home in a *Hard Rock*, no matter where in the world. It's a place where everyone is treated like a rock star, and people like to talk about the places they've been. My *Hard Rock* Bucharest t-shirt features a picture of *Bran Castle*.

After eating, I explored the city, walking the asphalt streets and stone-paved boulevards. My attention was caught by the *Opera House* steps, which are flanked by a pair of marble lions, and are overhung by an Art Deco stained glass awning fanning out over the sidewalk. The magnificent entranceway conjures a vision of a *fin de siècle* woman in a trailing beaded gown and gentleman in evening dress, sporting a top hat and gold-topped walking stick, being handed out of a coach-and-four to attend a performance. Wrought iron balconies and dormer windows with delectably carved details bear witness to elegance and wealth of times gone by.

City blocks are not uniform in Bucharest, where elegant

28

eighteenth-century buildings are scattered among communist-era structures with crumbling facades. The nearby *Ministry of the Interior* is a symmetrical grey stone building with many rows of windows, about eight stories without ornamentation—all business and no fun, befitting its communist origins.

The *Church of the Patriarchy* is an Ionic-columned white marble building with heavy wooden double doors. Stories from the Bible painted with Byzantine gold leaf embellish the porch walls in the front of the church. The gold reflects the sunlight and provides a striking contrast to the interior gloom. The church's shadowy interior is rich in the textural darkness of its green marble walls and mosaic tile floors, carved wood, Greek Orthodox icons, and profusion of brass chandeliers and filigree ornamentation. As I studied the church, I saw both tourists and the faithful milling around the sacred space, and several people made the sign of the cross; when I exited I spied older ladies in cotton aprons and babushkas walking in the street.

As I continued to explore on foot, I came to the Dambovita River, held in thrall by concrete flowing through the city, and I discovered a monument on *Revolution Square* that tells the Romanians' proud tale of their overthrow of communism. I walked through department stores like those back home and checked out the cocktail lounges of modern luxury hotels downtown.

In time I arrived at the *National Museum of Romanian History*, a beautiful turn-of the-century building which was to become my favorite museum. In it are the crown jewels, royal robes—fur-bordered sumptuous velvet mantles embroidered with gold, more akin to Genghis Khan's wardrobe than Henry Tudor's—and sumptuous riches of the Boyars and Dacians. This exotic museum of Eastern European history alone made the trip worthwhile.

The next day, after I had enjoyed an early morning constitutional, my driver picked me up in his car to take me to *Curtea Veche*, the court of Vlad the Impaler in Bucharest. I was following the trail of the Vlad, the Wallachian Voivode whose history inspired Bram

Stoker's depiction of Count Dracula. All that is left of the castle are the foundation and subterranean levels which are undergoing archaeological excavation. An iron fence surrounds the site. A bust of Vlad sits in the center where, my guide told me, the dungeons and torture chambers once were. A stone courtyard hemmed in by restaurants and shops adjoins the Count's lair.

The historical man I was in search of was Vlad III Dracul (1428–1477), the second son of Vlad II Dracul. The title "Dracul" refers to "Dragon," signifying the military order formed to halt Ottoman advances into Europe; and "Dracula" means "Son of the Dragon." As did the other fifteenth-century voivodes of Wallachia, Vlad II paid an annual tribute to the Ottomans, a sort of "protection money." (Wallachia, along with Transylvania and Moldavia, are the three regions of Romania). Even with the tribute money—in order to guarantee the obedience of Vlad II—the Sultan Mehmed II seized Vlad's sons Vlad III and Radu as hostages.

In 1447, Vlad II was deposed by the Hungarian John Hunyadi, and both he and his first-born son Mircea (Vlad III Dracul's older brother) were killed. Dracula was now one of several claimants to his father's throne.

Hunyadi was defeated by the Ottomans in 1448, and Vladislav II seized the Wallachian throne. At this point, Vlad joined with the Ottomans to retrieve the crown from Vladislav II.

At some later date, when he was Voivode, Dracula refused to pay the Sultan his tribute; in fact, he commanded the Sultan's emissaries be seized and impaled! The Sultan Mehmed was outraged, and he placed Radu on the Wallachian throne, deposing Dracula.

Vlad asked the Hungarian King Matthias Corvinus for his support; instead of helping him, though, Matthias threw Vlad into prison. After his release twelve years later in 1475, Vlad joined the Hungarian effort against the Ottomans. Vlad ruled as Voivode of Wallachia in three separate reigns—which were broken apart by continuous internal and external warfare—between 1448 and 1477.

Vlad's reputation for cruelty, for which he is known today, is chiefly the effect of the propaganda of the German monks, who publicized Dracula's heinous deeds by means of the latest technology in mass communication—the printing press. The monks could not print their pamphlets fast enough. The inclusion of a woodcut print of Vlad enjoying his dinner, seated at a formal table at his Forest of the Impaled, watching his victims slowly dying before him, made their Nurnberg pamphlet a best-seller. Vlad Dracul became known as Vlad Tepes (the Impaler) for his preferred method of execution.

Bards throughout the courts of Europe further circulated tales of Vlad's bloody and Machiavellian rule. They told tales of his forcing the boyars to build *Poenari Castle* with their own hands, and then ordering them impaled afterward.

Vlad had inaugurated his reign by purging thousands of boyars who had betrayed his murdered father and brother. He eliminated—by burning and impalement—hundreds of Saxon men, women, and children who had supported Vladislav II against him.

Notorious for a miraculous routing of the Sultan's superior army of one hundred fifty-thousand soldiers sent to depose him, Vlad's inspired defensive maneuver is known today as *The Forest of the Impaled*—a landscape of *twenty thousand people skewered alive on pikes planted into the ground*. The dead and dying were a sight that horrified the Turkish army, and it stopped them in their tracks.

From *Curtea Veche* my driver took me through both great streets and alleys of Bucharest which were lined with buildings representing the architectural styles of nearly a millennium. The water in one fountain on a city square was colored red—to advertise a vampire television show, my guide said.

We ended the second day at the *Outdoor Museum*, just outside of town, haven to lots of feral cats. The museum showcases traditional homes with decoratively woven thatched roofs and fences; some of these are braided like fancy women's hairdos, others like artisan baskets, in a variety of textures and patterns. Wooden gates tall enough to allow hay-laden wagons to pass through are adorned

31

with ornate carpentry. It is an exotic-feeling place to someone from more western regions.

On day three I checked out of the *Berthelot*: I had a new guide to drive me in a roughly circular route of about five hundred miles through Wallachia and Transylvania. We had not driven far before paved roads gave way to narrow, two-lane winding dirt roads, along which we frequently encountered horse and oxen-drawn wagons, very high and top-heavy with hay, coming around the blind curves. We passed sheep gathered by shepherds in common grazing areas. At frequent intervals were roadside shrines—little houses, like children's playhouses in backyards at home, painted in Byzantine icons and geometrical designs in the style of the borders of pages in Ottoman illuminated manuscripts. These travelers' shrines are surrounded by little wooden fences. A man wearing a cap and a vest over long-sleeved shirt, with walking stick in hand, watched us as we drove by. In some yards there were hay ricks taller than the houses, cone-shaped with small sheets of plastic on top. The houses are wood, stone, or concrete and simple, mostly one-story. The Carpathian Mountains loom over them in the distance.

We arrived at the *Curtea De Arges*, the ruins of Vlad's first princely court; all that remains of it is the foundation, swept clean by archaeologists' brushes. Next to it is a medieval Byzantine tomb, the burial place of the Royal Family of Romania, the resting place of Wallachian and Transylvanian royalty from nearly a thousand years ago. The tomb's interior walls are covered with dark frescoes featuring God, the saints, and stories from the Stations of the Cross, the colors smoky with time and the residue of oil lamps and candles. The silver chandeliers were lighted for us, but it was still dark. Herein is the tomb of Vladislav I Vlacu (1364-1372) and other forebears of the Impaler. The little light there is bounces off the gold leaf of the icons on the walls. Behind a silk rope, in an alcove, is an altar on which sits a gold Eastern Orthodox cross. Some parts of the frescoes and sculpted words have been obliterated, the result of the dampness of generations, and probably also destruction by those who triumphed over them in the centuries of unremitting warfare.

It was jarring to emerge from the oppression of the tomb into the daylight: the bloody past still clung thickly to me as I looked at the row of 1970s block buildings, with flaking facades (in a much worse state of disrepair than many of the buildings of previous centuries) which faced the *Curtea De Arges*. Between the tomb and the road stood a statue of Basarab I, the voivode of Wallachia and the founder of Dracula's dynasty, another strange juxtaposition. Basarab's was a commanding stance. He seemed sadly out of place. His time had long since gone.

From the royal court and the tomb, we drove to the *Monastery at the Curtea De Arges*. It is an exquisite wedding-cake building of white marble with grey marble details. From a distance it is a cube with a canopy-style main entrance, the canopy fashioned of marble, over an arched doorway; three minaret-style crowns sit on top, the center one octagonal and sitting higher than the two on either side of it, which are cylindrical. The spires atop the crowns are brass Byzantine three-armed crosses. As we drew near, I saw that the surface of the whole is covered with delicate marble filigree in intricate and fine lace-like patterns.

At day's end we reached Brasov, and I went in search of dinner and souvenir shopping. But first I registered at my hotel and unpacked. The hotel was on the same square shown in the movie *Transylvania 6-5000*; it was here I stayed for the three nights I was in Transylvania. The whole town is made of brick and stone buildings, my hotel among them, joined together in the manner of townhouses. Situated in a fertile green basin of the towering Carpathian Mountains, adjoining buildings in the fifteenth century would have served as fortifications as well as businesses and homes. Eighteenth-century and medieval buildings commingle, and the *Black Church* (which is really white and grey marble) is at the town center. The church is still in use, and a tour will take you into its bowels where piles of bones are stored.

The destination of the next day was the town in which Vlad Dracul was born, Sighisoara, seventy-five miles to the northwest of Brasov. The streets are stone-paved, and there is a gate, a watchtower entrance to the walled city, a common feature of most medieval towns. Rows of adjoining buildings delineate the square. A plaque marks the yellow building which was the home of Vlad Dracul. There my guide and I had soup and bread for lunch (it is now a restaurant), eating at tables with decorative wooden chairs of a very distinctive Eastern European style. The ceilings have wrought iron chandeliers. I posed for a picture with my arm around a bust of Vlad. I am never less than amazed that medieval buildings are still in use all over Europe, and I feel that eating and sleeping, working and shopping in them enables me to comprehend history as a living process, not a singular event.

As we drove up into the mountains, I saw that every place we had been dwindled to Lilliputian size, and rivers became thin lines; cars on roads seemed the size of ants from my new perspective. The Carpathians are rocky and very high, and thickly forested. It being October, the mountain foliage was of parti-colored oranges, greens, reds, and yellows, although when I looked down, I saw that the valley still retained its green hue. At a restaurant and lodge my guide stopped the car and said we had arrived at *Poenari,* once a stronghold of Vlad Dracul. The guide was not going up, as he had been several times.

I began my climb doing two steps at a time, to get there faster, but that didn't last long. There are fifteen hundred steps up a steep grade, and it took me ninety minutes to get to the top of the mountain. Halfway up, the multi-story lodge looked like a *Monopoly* hotel. The climb was beautiful. The thick vegetation, the bird's eye view, and the destination ahead were sublime. At the top, which literally touched the clouds, I met a couple from South Carolina, and another from Ontario. There were maybe a dozen people there.

The remains of *Poenari* Castle rest atop the summit of a mountain. War and earthquakes have eradicated most of the castle, but some walls remain. The Romanian flag flies above the ramparts, and the slopes around the castle are marked by several impaled mannequins with *blood* running down the pikes on which they are skewered, a nod to *The Forest of the Impaled*. Today Vlad Dracul is revered as a national hero by the Romanian people, as the man who did the most effective job of keeping the Turks out of Europe and defending Christianity from the Ottomans; Transylvania and Wallachia were always left holding the frontier between Europe and the East when the Crusading kings of Western Europe failed to show up to do battle.

After traipsing all over the ruins, using up several rolls of film in an effort to capture this experience forever, I began the descent, which was much easier. It had not been a difficult climb, just a lengthy one. While gravity made the descent less taxing than the ascent, the grade required holding onto the handrail on the way down.

Two additional castles were on the agenda. En route from Bucharest to *Curtea De Arges* we had made a short visit to *Bran Castle* (the one featured on my *Hard Rock* shirt), a more or less intact medieval castle which is often referred to as "Castle Dracula," and which had served as a customs station along the road in Vlad Dracul's time, but was not a castle inhabited by him, as was *Poenari;* it is used in movies regularly. It is a bare, stone fortress with smoothly finished walls. The many small rooms of the castle are reached by narrow, winding corridors and have tiny windows. Now, as we drove the last part of the circle bringing me back to Bucharest (and the airport), we visited another castle—*Peles* Castle, a late nineteenth-century castle in the sumptuous German neo-Renaissance style with beautiful Saxon woodcarving throughout, ornamenting the dark wood of the interior.

I observed ancient Roman and Dacian ruins, visible here and there, left and right from the road all along the route that we traced through the heart of Romania. Many peoples had trod this soil, and lived and died upon it, and I felt once more that existence is eternal and organic, not a matter of discreet occurrences.

My search for Dracula ended at his tomb in the fourteenth-century monastery of Snagov, on a small island in the middle of a lake by the same name. The monastery is small and square, and constructed of stones of variegated shades of white and tan and brown and is topped with a small cylindrical tower. There is a park in front, and a bridge connects the island to the mainland, which is a residential area close to the city of Bucharest. The monks collect entry fees and charge for the privilege of taking pictures. The interior is dark red and green marble with large gold candelabra.

In 1477 Vlad Dracul died in battle against the Ottomans, his corpse reportedly cut into pieces and his head presented to Mehmed. Nineteenth-century historians maintained that his remains were interred at Snagov. Vlad Dracul's burial place, a placard purports, is beneath a marble slab on the floor. My guide said that when an attempt was made to exhume Vlad, all that was found there were horses' bones and purple cloth. That should not have been a surprise. National hero notwithstanding, an empty tomb is a sure sign that its one-time occupant is Un-Dead and at-large.

I tried to sear these memories into my brain as I thanked my driver and boarded a plane for my next stop—Vienna, where I would spend the next five days at a hotel near the *Schoenbrunn Palace*. From Vienna I would be making an expedition by rail through the countryside of Hungary to Budapest, to see the country my father's parents had lived in before they emigrated as children to America (they had entered the United States through Ellis Island when the twentieth century was young). While I was certain to make wonderful memories in those cities, I knew it was going to be very difficult to surpass the exhilaration I felt walking in the footsteps of Dracula, Sovereign of the Undead.

I mpatiently, I threaded my way through the modern business and shopping streets of Edinburgh, Scotland. It was early morning, and I had just arrived on an express train from London. I had left most of my luggage in London and come to Edinburgh with my camera and a change of clothes, to spend a day and a night there, and to return to London the next morning. Emerging from the modern district where the train station was, I came to a green park. It was September and still warm, and a good number of people were enjoying the day, walking along the paths or sitting on benches and talking. Beyond the park I saw a hill, on top of which was a castle. I asked some local people for directions and turned my steps that way.

Old Edinburgh is on top of the volcanic promontory known as Castle Rock. It is a steep walk up the stone-paved streets to the Royal Mile, which is a wondrous shopping and dining gauntlet 'twixt the Palace of Holyrood House at one end and Edinburgh Castle at the other. I checked into my hotel on the Mile and was back on the street as fast as I could stow my overnight bag. My hotel was in the center of the Royal Mile, and I determined to walk to Holyrood House and then proceed to Edinburgh Castle, sampling all the shops and some Scottish delicacies along the way.

Approaching Holyrood House, the first thing that the visitor discerns is that it is a somewhat square-shaped castle, circular crenelated towers with coned roofs at the four corners, reminiscent of rooks in a chess set. Symmetrically laid out, four sides around an open court, it is built of brown and gray stone, numerous chimneys rising from its roof against the deep blue sky, filled with white cumulus clouds that day. Along the walls are numerous niches framing statuary. It is the home of Queen Elizabeth when she is in Scotland. Before the main entrance is a hexagonal swath of grass surrounding a tall stone fountain in the center of a large paved courtyard that is framed by an elaborate wrought iron fence. The inner courtyard is a lawn of green grass surrounded by a covered walkway. Two stories of windows rest on the portico, and on the top-most floor are dormer windows.

The interior is viewed with a tour guide, who leads the way through sumptuous rooms of richly paneled walls and gilt furnishings. Royal treasures abound throughout, and the portrait gallery is a grand room of state that features portraits of all the Scottish rulers, Macbeth included. Weapons, arms, and tapestries cover the walls. The ceilings are works of art in their own right. The climax of the tour is the bedroom of Mary, Queen of Scots, and the adjoining chamber wherein her husband's men killed her confidante David Rizzio; her cabinet houses her collection of bibelots, worth a Queen's ransom.

The best part of Holyrood, though, is the crumbling twelfth-century abbey next to the castle. The sky is visible through gothic windows lacking the stained glass that used to be there. Gothic arches abound in the four outer walls remaining, and pillars stand in the grassy center, holding up the sky, as the roof has long since ceased to exist. Ruined gothic abbeys are much more satisfying than intact, albeit beautiful, palaces. The spirit, the sense of adventure, takes flight from these stone heuristics. As visitors meander around the space, examining doorways and niches, they begin to imagine life when the abbey was intact, to people the spaces in their own minds, to make up their own stories, and to fill the grounds with spectres from their own imaginations.

Leaving Holyrood behind, I made my way up the narrow winding street, enjoying coffee and shortbread in a sidewalk café along the way; and then I had a taste of Scotch whiskey in a pub, served by a bartender in a pressed white shirt, sleeves rolled up at the elbows, and a black vest. Window-shopping afforded the prospect of male mannequins in tartans and kilts, and luxurious woolen sweaters and outerwear. On either side of the street, I spied small passages ("closes") between the buildings. Where there is a gap in the architecture, I could see how high up I was from the point at which I had disembarked the train, high above the treetops of the park I had encountered on my arrival.

En route to Edinburgh Castle, I came to St. Giles Cathedral, a tall, dark gothic structure, in the center of the old town. Home of the Presbyterian Church, stone angels watch over the visitors beneath the flying buttresses overhead, as people peer into all the side nooks and crannies, marveling at the art and architecture. Large stained glasses allow red, blue, and green colors to flood the space.

The gothic theme is enlarged upon at the neighboring *Witchery by the Castle* restaurant. A brass plaque on the exterior wall reads that Boswell and Johnson "dined in this building circa 1770." The dining room is below ground. Looking down at it from the top of the stairs is bewitching: the room is ornately gothic, with arches, stone walls, wrought iron chandeliers, and on each white cloth-covered table is a prominent brass candlestick that seems to have been taken directly from off a cathedral altar. At dinner the room is entirely candle-lit, making it difficult to read the menu, but heightening the sense of mystery and adventure. The food and service are extraordinary. *The Witchery* also offers suites with ecclesiastical gothic seasoning, a la Horace Walpole, Ann Radcliffe, and, of course, Sir Walter Scott; in one the double bath is hidden behind a secret door that doubles as a library bookcase, and throughout the décor is red velvet with gold, and dark wood. One would expect a maniacal abbot to imprison a shrinking virgin herein, who awaited delivery by her brave knight. I made my dinner reservation there for the end of the day.

Continuing uphill along the narrow street, I encountered a

bagpiper in full tartan regalia, who kindly allowed me to have my picture taken with him (at least I think he assented—he couldn't really speak with the pipe in his mouth). I visited the Huntley House Museum, a restored sixteenth-century building. I passed caricature artists and more musicians along the road.

Edinburgh Castle is massive, built out of the rocky crag, its entryway a wide stone-paved passage, through a gate with bars that can be raised and lowered. It is an amalgam of parts, unlike the symmetrical unity of Holyrood House. Circular walls abut square angles. Lang Stairs, a central, stone, winding staircase begs for photos. Stone-carved medieval soldiers and royalty stand guard in their niches. The Great Hall rises about as high as its hammer-beam ceiling can go. Rich, warm wood paneling covers the walls up to about twelve feet from the floor and is covered with arms and armor. The walls are red above the paneling, and medieval pikes are arrayed in fan-like arrangements about them. At least twenty people could stand together in the huge fireplace. There is a part of the castle dedicated to the history of Scotland, with wax figures and live actors telling the story of Mary, Queen of Scots, and other rulers; along the wall is a medieval-looking gold-leaf timeline, an illuminated manuscript on the wall. Below the castle is the Military Prison, where the visitor can learn about the life of the prisoners held there over the centuries. The Crown Jewels of Scotland are the end of the journey, the treasury of a nation, portable wealth and dazzling visible insignias of power. Coming into the sunlight again, I saw a wedding in progress, the bride in white satin and lace, and the groom and his party in kilts, white hose, and shoes that lace up the calves. I took High Tea in the Tea Room.

I had one more adventure awaiting me before dinner at *The Witchery*: *Mary King's Close* beneath the town. In the fifteenth and sixteenth centuries, the Edinburgh population had been steadily increasing, and as the city was on a cliff and surrounded by a twenty-three foot-tall city wall erected because of the frequent battles with the English, Edinburgh built itself up instead of out, into high tenement buildings. When they could no longer build up, they built down, basements below basements, building sideways into the rock, creating subterranean tenements excavated in cold, wet, rock.

This was housing for the poorest folk. Of course, disease was rampant, with rats, no ventilation to let fire smoke out or fresh air in, and steep passages to the street to remove refuse or obtain water. Building fires was dangerous, too, as eight or ten stories of wooden structures rested on the underground apartments. The sewage system back then involved tossing refuse into the street (after politely calling, "Gardy Loo," to warn pedestrians), and the sewage covering the streets would leak down into the closes. These underground tenements could have been entered from a street-level door and then down some stairs (similar to entering the lower level of a split-level building), but the Great Fire of 1824 and the collapse of tenement buildings in the nineteenth-century brought about the demolition of the high-rises and the filling-in of cellars, and the erection of new buildings upon them. In 1994 the excavated streets (closes) of the buried rubble were re-opened to the public, among them *Mary King's Close*.

Mary King's Close is a good place for ghost-hunters, for there are many sad stories to be heard here, of the people who lived underground. The tour to the "town beneath the street," as it is called, dramatizes these piteous tales. *Mary King's Close* is a damp, dark, claustrophobic place, where mannequins live and work several stories below ground. The Plague Doctor is a frequent visitor, with his beaked mask filled with sweet-smelling herbs to protect him from *miasma* (vapors which were believed to cause illness) in the days before germ theory. The Plague nearly wiped out the population of crowded Edinburgh in the seventeenth century, and officials resorted to sealing up the sick in their homes, effectively burying them alive. For a long time, *Mary King's Close* was supposed to have been one of the sealed tenements, but recent research has disproved that. Yet, sightings of ghosts and unexplained lights are still frequently reported, and the close has maintained its notoriety for being haunted for nearly four centuries.

It was dark when I came up to the gift shop at street level, and I walked toward *The Witchery* for my gothic abbey dinner. The shadowy candle-lit subterranean dining room was an appropriate finale to a gothic Edinburgh day. I would not have been surprised to find myself in a room filled with elegantly dressed vampires celebrating their hunt, for they, too, would feel quite at home in this elegant hideaway.

Phantom of the Paris Opera House

I had been to Harrod's that day, where I had champagne in the Champagne Bar, and High Tea in the restaurant, and shopped most of the day. Among the goods purveyed in that most venerated establishment was a Lladro figurine of an Egyptian pleasure barge filled with dancing ladies and shaved-headed youths, as large as a banquet table for twelve; and a grand piano covered in green stone (malachite?) and gilt ormolus caught my eye. A gracious salesclerk demonstrated for me how to put up my hair with a very expensive comb, which price I considered a fair rate for the hairdressing lesson. I had also been to *Fortnum and Mason's*, where they offered me champagne, which fortified me for further shopping. In fact, I shopped and tea-ed and champagne-d away the day, until it was time to take a cab to *The Phantom of the Opera*. With my new coiffure and my new big black Prada sunglasses from Harrod's, I felt like Holly Go Lightly as the doorman helped me into a taxi. I had seen *Phantom* thrice in Toronto, once in Las Vegas, and now, at last, in London.

Andrew Lloyd Webber's masterpiece is worth enjoying over and over. My heart thrills to *Masquerade* and *Music of the Night*, and I cry out a silent warning to Christine when the Phantom tutors her through her dressing room mirror. But—oh!—when the stage becomes the underground lair of the Phantom, when the subterranean lake rises and the candelabra eerily glow, and when the Phantom guides his boat with Christine on board to his lair—the effect is electrifying! Webber skillfully evokes romantic and horrific emotions through his music in combination with the sublime visual experience of the costumes and sets of menacing beauty. I await the next opportunity to descend into that world once more.

The next morning, after a good night's sleep at my hotel, I rose early to take the Chunnel to Paris. It is a journey beneath the English Channel of only a couple of hours, and it cost me less than a hundred dollars to traipse between the two capitals. The Chunnel ride is mostly dark tunnel, during which time I did some reading, and the time passed quickly. I arrived at the Paris Nord train station, a huge, airy, barn-like building where trains on many tracks load and unload their passengers.

I hailed a cab for the premier destination on the day's agenda: The Paris Opera House. With the London production of the previous night still fresh in my mind, I felt as if I were about to enter that world of horrific pleasure, and I exited the taxi and stood before the beautiful white stone Opera House. Seven arched arcades offer street-level entrances to the lobby. The next level above has seven loggias with Corinthian pillars, and over that is a third level decorated around with a wreath of drama masks, and sculptural groups on each corner of the roof. A dome of copper verdigris and gold trim crowns the whole, with a sculptural group of Apollo, Dance, and Music at the peak. Mere words cannot describe the delicate beauty of the Second Empire details. The French, by their gift for combining richness with delicacy in a way unique to themselves, have given the world some of the most elegant splendor it has known.

The interior rivals Versailles for the title of the most beautiful building on earth. Entering, one sees the grand staircase of white marble, which divides into two at the landing. Black Art Noveau sculptures at the base hold multiple candelabra. The staircase is carved in a profusion of marble flowers and ribbon, no space left undecorated. The theatergoer is surrounded by multiple levels of carved marble balconies and arches, and chandeliers and candelabra, reflected light sparkling off the white marble and gold surfaces. Beneath the small rotunda is a fountain; a person standing there is almost entombed by marble—floor, ceiling, pillars, and statuary surrounding the relatively intimate space. It is apparent that the Opera House itself is a theater set—an opulent stage on which the patrons could play out their own pageants of social ambition and political plotting.

The main foyer is a great hall with marble floors and gold walls. Baroque paintings punctuated with ornate golden frames cover the ceilings. Double fluted columns leafed in gold detail the walls. Dozens of gilt chandeliers are suspended from the sumptuous ceiling. Red velvet and gold swath the auditorium, where three rows of boxes encircle the stage; and a *trompe l'oeil* painting of a rich red velvet curtain hangs on the stage. How many political plots and romantic assignations were played out in these boxes, where the *crème de la crème* of society gathered to mingle, and to be seen? The Opera House functioned more as an assembly room than an entertainment venue, a place for intrigue and gossip, lending itself to the creation of legends like the Phantom of the Opera and other mysterious entities in its bowels beneath the earth, its secret passages and subterranean waterways. The legends that have grown up around the Paris Opera House reflect the treacherous maneuvers of the patrons within.

The tour concluded with a visit to the luxuriously paneled, two story Opera House library, in which can be found miniature stage sets and dioramas of many past performances. When I left the Opera House, I headed to the nearest sidewalk café for a glass of chardonnay and a little repast, while I calculated how much time I had remaining before I needed to board the train back to London. After lunch, I walked along the Seine, enjoying the beautiful bridges over the flowing river and its *fin de siècle* street lamps. I window-shopped designer boutiques and could have wept to leave behind a Dolce and Gabana gold lame dress with a medieval gothic motif. I saw mopeds parked in front of the Dior shop. I took a bicycle rickshaw ride to the Louvre and walked around the square, admiring the Baroque palaces and the glass pyramid in the center. I enjoyed the beautiful gardens of the Tuileries, where people were feeding pigeons and taking selfies. I posed for a picture by the Eiffel Tower, and I turned down a gentleman's offer to rent a Lamborghini in the Place de la Concorde. "Poor Marie Antoinette," Carlyle's lament resonates with me. *J'adore Marie Antoinette*, who for me is the patron saint of beauty, of the heights that can be reached through splendor in architecture and divinity in interiors. Here, in the Place de la Concorde, she was beheaded. Here also is the obelisk from the Temple of Luxor given France by the Viceroy of Egypt in 1831, a poignant reminder of the fall of great civilizations, and of the brevity of life.

As I boarded the Eurostar at the Paris Nord, I thought of the two opera houses. The real one is infamous for beauty, grandeur, and human passion and intrigue, and the fictional for the monster who reflects the horrors we face from each other. *Au revoir*, City of Light.

Whitby, Where Dracula Came to England

$\mathcal{E}$arly one May morning I boarded the train for Whitby, England, as did Bram Stoker when he embarked upon his holiday. I changed trains twice during that excursion from London. The third train I rode, which left me at the Whitby station, was an old one that went *clickety-clack*. Independent of its destination, the excursion itself was a delightful experience—a rail ride through the heart of England, journeying over rolling farmlands and green meadows which separate cities and towns, through pastures where scores of sheep grazing look like cotton puffs on an emerald ground, through the marshlands of the northernmost limits of the realm, and eventually arriving at the rocky northeast coast, where blue skies with wispy white clouds meet the deeper blue of the North Sea. It was at the Whitby Harbor that Dracula came to England, aboard the *Demeter*—that cursed ship arrived in storm and fury to bring havoc to this quaint seaside town, and to England. This is the same coastal vill at which Bram Stoker and Lewis Carroll once enjoyed their holidays.

The May sky was variable that day, at times light blue, and grey at other times. I hurried from the train station to the harbor, which bisects the town, and I walked toward the East Cliff. I was anxious to see the abbey and graveyard which had inspired Bram Stoker; he used to sit on a bench on the West Cliff, and he would look past the harbor to the East Cliff, where the ruins of the cathedral provided material for his fertile brain. I ascended the steep, winding street, but my progress was significantly slowed by the tightly packed or adjoining buildings, narrow and of two or three

47

stories, most of which pre-dated Stoker's time. There were shops (!) with mesmeric powers and restaurants and pubs. At the *Marie Antoinette* patisserie, I had coffee and a scone. I resolved to wait until the way down to shop in the numerous boutiques.

Scurrying up the one hundred ninety-nine steps, I passed St. Mary's graveyard on the very edge of the cliff on the North Sea, and I passed St. Mary's Church and the Whitby Cathedral (in magnificent skeletal condition). I glanced back at the many red tile roofs of the houses below stairs, and I saw that I was level with the West Coast across the harbor. I continued hurriedly until I reached the Whitby Abbey museum where—after quickly reviewing the history of Whitby (which includes the history of Captain Cook, of whaling, and the mining of jet) and having made a rapid tour of the museum's fine arts and costume collections—I hastened back to savor the Dracula experience at the Whitby Cathedral, for which I had crossed the Atlantic Ocean.

I love crumbling cathedrals, Gothic arches, Celtic crosses, medieval stone walls, grass where stone floors should have been—and so I explored the crannies and posed for snapshots, exhilarated as a little girl in a playhouse. I climbed steps that no longer led anywhere and looked though doors that opened to eternity. In the seventh century on this site was the monastery where the Northumbrian poet Caedmon lived; in the ninth century the monastery was destroyed by the Danes. It was rebuilt in the eleventh century under William the Conqueror. I envisioned the cathedral as it was when sixteenth-century worshipers in the sacristy heard of Henry VIII's assault on the monasteries—which was the final death knell to the Whitby Cathedral. I imagined, too, vampires and ghosts waiting for lone women like myself, who came here and *just waited*. I exhilarated in my moment on the ocean cliff, where the sea wind was nippy and exciting, and it was with reluctance that I turned my back on the gaunt cathedral remnants which had inspired Stoker's *Carfax Abbey*.

I walked toward the graveyard of St. Mary's Church: here Lucy and Mina used to talk with the old man about suicides' graves and deaths at sea, and worried about the great dog which had run away after the *Demeter* had come ashore. Most of the texts on the headstones have been eroded away by wind and rain. They lean at all kinds of odd angles. A graveyard on the sea cliff, a ruined cathedral at my back, tall grasses blowing in the wind—this last hour at the windswept coast of Whitby made my trans-Atlantic voyage worth every bit of the effort. Now I look at my photos and I am there again, in the Middle Ages, and with Lucy Westenra and Mina Harker, in the shadow of the approaching Dracula.

Resigned to the fact that I could not remain in that grave-yard forever, I descended the one hundred ninety-nine steps and explored the bustling trade center. The narrow medieval streets are packed with people jostling elbows as they move. I drank a draught English ale at a pub ("When in England...") and made a purchase in a quaint little jewelry shop—a jet necklace. Jet is mined here and, ever since Queen Victoria and her mania for the funerary, jet has been a staple of mourners and lately of the Goth set. The jet pendant, mined and made in Whitby, will always be a treasured memento to me, resurrecting my experience whenever I fasten it on my neck.

I walked down to the harbor and took a photo of an eigh-teenth-century naval officer on the waterfront, and then I walked up the steps to the West Cliff. I asked a dozen people until I found one who could direct me to Bram Stoker's bench. Lo and behold!—there it was—with a plaque proclaiming that "the view from this seat inspired Bram Stoker (1847–1912) to use Whitby as the setting of part of the world-famous novel *Dracula*." My view of the graveyard and abbey across the harbor was the same as Bram Stoker's view. Once again, I found myself with one foot in the past and one in the present. I sat on the bench and let it all sink in and become part of me, another remarkable experience to be integrated into myself.

After a time, I walked past the statue of Captain Cook on the

West Cliff: Cook was born in a nearby town, and his ship the *Bark Endeavor*, had been built in Whitby. I also passed the Whalebone Arch, a tribute to the nineteenth-century whaling industry of Whitby. I walked from here to townhouses on a crescent, reminding me of Bath; Lucy and Mina had stayed in one of these. Plaques marked the buildings in which Bram Stoker and Lewis Carroll had spent their seaside holidays, as well.

As evening came, I had to board the train for the return trip to London. There were many places yet to explore during my sojourn in England, and even one more Dracula experience: the Hard Rock Café in London is on the site which was one of Dracula's London addresses.

Henry VIII is a fascinating man. His notoriety as a serial husband to six wives initially garners people's interest; then, as they learn more about the stories of his nuptials, they realize that Henry's marital marathon is a series of political intrigues. His marriages spell the story of a powerful man's determination to demonstrate —by skewed reason and agile rationalizations—that not only was he King by divine right, but also arbiter of the conscience of each and every Englishman (Henry had usurped the role of Head of the English Church from the Pope, inaugurating the Reformation in England). The uxorious monarch was an incredibly complex man who could perform all manner of intellectual maneuvers to justify adultery, incest, murder, perjury, and betrayal in the name of God. I made my journey to Hampton Court and the Tower of London to spend time considering Henry VIII and a Tudor England that was confused, having barely emerged from the Middle Ages into the Renaissance of Erasmus and More.

Hampton Court was a gift from Henry VIII to his favorite Cardinal Thomas Wolsey, which was subsequently returned to the King when Wolsey—having failed to obtain for his liege lord an annulment from his inconvenient marriage to Catherine of Aragon—fell from favor in 1529. Anne Boleyn's Gate revealed itself to me first, as I approached Hampton Court on foot from the train station. Anne Boleyn's Gate had been added to Hampton Court during Henry's renovations in 1540. (Later, under William of Orange, Hampton Court was subjected to significant Baroque modifications by Christopher Wren). On the bridge over the moat before the gate are a menagerie of ten statues of ancestral animals—the unicorn of Scotland and the crowned lion of England who gnashes his teeth, among them—each bears a shield emblazoned with heraldic symbols—fleur de lis, thistles, lions.

Hampton Court is an imposing castle with vast chambers in which Henry would assemble his more than a thousand courtiers. Prodigious tapestries covering the stone walls provided insulation from the winter winds blowing in between the chinks of the cold castle. The Great Hall is a massive dining hall with a hammer beam roof; at the top of the high walls are stained glass windows which alternate with antlers. The grand staircase has rails of ornamental wrought iron, and on the surrounding walls are paintings in the classical allegory style of the Renaissance, their bright blues and reds relieving the monotone of grey stone. The fireplace in the enormous kitchen has space enough for parking several mini vans; it was here the kitchen staff would prepare refreshment for Henry and his retinue when Henry honored Cardinal Wolsey with a visit during one of his progresses. There are no intimate spaces in this part of the castle, where private life gave way to public performance.

Passing through a massive doorway, I found myself face-to-face with a corpulent Henry VIII, his own bulk increased by fur mantles and robes of embroidered velvet and satin, over which were hanging thick and heavy gold chains. He was surrounded by a bevy of obsequious courtiers, among whom was flitting an agitated Anne Boleyn. She was protesting to one and all her innocence, declaring herself to be an honest and faithful wife. The King ignored Anne, and when he passed out from the chamber he joined a modest Jane Seymour, with whom he departed the company, leaving Anne to the tittering of the court. Unfortunately for the faithless Anne Boleyn, her story did not end there. The royal personages were easily recognizable, their costumes drawn from Holbein's portraits. Some of Henry's wives still live at Hampton Court, it seems. Jane Seymour, third wife to Henry, has been seen hanging about Hampton Court, where she died giving birth to Henry's son Edward. Also sighted is Catherine Howard, wife number five, who was executed for adultery before her twentieth birthday.

I followed the trail of Henry's doomed second wife to the Tower of London by means of a water taxi. I boarded the motorboat on the bank of the Thames River at Greenwich, where I verified the accuracy of my watch against Greenwich Mean Time. The Prime Meridian passes through Greenwich, and I took the opportunity to stand with one foot in the Eastern Hemisphere and the other in the Western Hemisphere. The old Royal Observatory here had been commissioned in 1675 by Charles II. The buildings, designed by Christopher Wren, are now museums, the scientific work having been moved elsewhere.

Greenwich is built right up to the riverbank, whence I was carried by water taxi past Big Ben and the London Ferris Wheel, and under the Blackfriars' Bridge to the Tower Bridge and the Tower of London. On the north bank of the Thames River two crenellated walls and a moat surround a complex of buildings that make up the Tower of London. A sign posted where the water taxi approached reads: *Entry to the Traitors' Gate.* The Tower of London was built for use as a royal castle between 1066 and 1078, the period of the Norman Conquest, but served as administrative buildings and a prison from 1100 until 1952. Not only Anne Boleyn, but also Catherine Howard, Lady Jane Grey (nine days' Queen of England until dethroned by Queen Mary in 1553), Elizabeth I (also imprisoned by Queen Mary before she took the throne), Sir Walter Raleigh, Sir Thomas More, and the Little Princes imprisoned by Richard III were held in the Tower.

I walked the battlements and peeked into the towers and corridors and came to the re-created bedchamber of Edward I Plantagenet (1239–1307). His bed is on a raised wooden platform. A pole in each corner of the platform supports the curtains that would have been pulled around the bed for warmth and privacy. The fireplace hearth is tiled in decorative squares of blue and white. Candles are in wrought iron sconces.

Since 1661 the Crown Jewels have been stored in the Tower of London. Symbols of the British Monarchy, they are recognizable to people around the world. When not in use (for ceremonial purposes) they are stored in the Tower and on display for visitors. Coronation regalia used since the 1100s and insignia used for the Opening of Parliament are exhibited with explanations of their ritual functions. St. Edward's Crown is the crown that is placed upon the head of the new monarch during the Coronation ceremony. The Imperial State Crown is the crown the new King or Queen wears in the Procession out of Westminster Abbey. Other crowns, swords, trumpets, maces, scepters, orbs, rings, and treasures used at the altar during coronations and baptisms are kept here.

Medieval weapons are displayed in the Tower, typical among them a yeoman mannequin dressed in leather and brass mail with a pike and a knight clad in steel armor on a horse. Outside the walls of the castle is a functioning catapult. The Traitors' Gate at the moat, raised and lowered by ropes and pulleys, was the one-way turnstile for condemned prisoners brought to the Tower for their execution. Among the torture devices on display is a Rack, and a device called the "Scavenger's Daughter," a round metal disk on which a prisoner was forced to kneel with his head down to his knees and his arms folded against his chest. As does a handle on a basket, two iron arcs came together over the prisoner's haunches and met over his lower back; these were joined together and tightened until bones were broken and blood flowing from his orifices gave evidence of internal injuries. Most of the interrogated would have confessed to the crimes of which they had been accused, knowing that still they would die, but wanting to relieve the immediate pain. There are many visitors and staff at the Tower of London who claim that the cries of the tortured are still heard of a night.

Anne Boleyn is said to appear at night—carrying her head. The place of her beheading is marked with a marble tile surmounted by a disk of blue glass. The words carved on the memorial read:

Gentle visitor pause a while, where you stand death cut away the light of many days. Here jeweled names were broken from the vivid thread of life. May they rest in peace while we walk the generations around their strife and courage, under these restless skies.

Anne has been sighted at the Church of St. Paul ad Vincula, which is within the Tower complex and which is where her body was buried. Lady Jane Grey and the Little Princes have also been seen. The Tower is distinguished for its orbs and paranormal activity, as would be expected where so many were tortured and died.

Beefeaters, or Yeoman Warders, are very gracious about tourists' requests for photos. They have been the royal bodyguard since the fifteenth century. As I was gazing at Anne Boleyn's marker, one of the Beefeaters shared with me the legend of the Ravens of the Tower of London. He said that by decree of Charles II the ravens of the Tower are to be protected, for the King had received a warning that the kingdom would fall if the ravens left the Tower. The Ravenkeeper minds the ravens, who have the freedom of the Tower grounds.

I boarded the water taxi for dinner, the last stop on that day's itinerary, my heart full of emotion, having spent the day in the life of Henry VIII and Anne Boleyn, and the ghosts who walk Hampton Court and the Tower of London.

Mysterious Stonehenge

Stonehenge represents Mystery—not mystery as in an Agatha Christie detective story—but as in the unknown in the Cosmos. Five millennia ago some people constructed a great stone circle. Archaeologists, scientists, historians, and a lot of the rest of us want to know what their purpose was and how they did it. In search of these answers, we consider why *we* build things—we build homes for shelter, offices to work at for gain, auditoriums in which to gather for business and for pleasure, public places to worship or commemorate—and we cannot imagine what Neolithic people wanted to accomplish that required such a monumental undertaking. What would prompt people to move two-ton stones 150 miles before the invention of the wheel?

I was using London as a hub for a two weeks' holiday, traipsing about Britain to see places I knew very well already from books and film. To see Stonehenge, I took an excursion by tour bus from London to Bath and Stonehenge.

I had spent one full day in Bath already on this vacation, immersing myself in Jane Austen and Georgian and Regency landmarks. Serendipitously, I had found myself in the midst of the annual *Jane Austen Festival*, and there were Mr. Darcy's and Eliza Bennett's everywhere I turned. *The Jane Austen Center* and its *Regency Tea Room* provide vital logistical information about Bath. Within the *Jane Austen Center* is a delightful little museum paying homage to Austen and the Regency Period. I bought an *I♥Darcy* bumper sticker and enjoyed a cup of tea in the *Regency Tea Room*; afterward, I proceeded to the nearby *Museum of Costume*, a treasure trove of historic garments. I walked around *The Royal Crescent*, taking a tour of *Number One, The Royal Crescent*, a townhouse turned museum of late eighteenth-century genteel living in fashionable Bath. I visited the *Assembly Room* and had a light luncheon in the *Grand Pump Room*, where being seen was rather more important than dining or even taking the waters in Jane Austen's time. I crossed the *Pultney Bridge* and then stopped at the exquisite, jewel-box *Bath Abbey* where Jane Austen attended church when she lived in Bath. A cruciform gothic Bath (yellow) stone edifice in a stone square lined with benches, the white marble fan vaulting interior is stunning. The memorial wall and floor plaques, with the prism effects of the stained-glass windows that cover eighty percent of the wall space, render the splendid church a colorful and intimate space compared to some of the more somberly majestic cathedrals. The Roman Baths I reserved for a later visit.

Two days later, I returned to Bath on another bus tour which included Stonehenge. I was journeying not only from city into country, but also backwards into time. In Bath I explored the Roman Baths beneath the Regency landmarks I had earlier savored. From geothermal springs under the streets of Bath heated water rises through the Pennyquick fault and provides clean, potable spa water. Archaeology provides evidence that the waters have been considered beneficial since Celtic times.

The Roman invasion resulted in the first-century A.D. construction of a temple at the spring dedicated to the Celtic goddess Sulis. The Temple was expanded over the next two centuries, but the complex later fell into disuse when the Roman occupation ended in the fifth century. After the withdrawal of Rome, the baths were subsequently rebuilt several times. Currently the baths remain in the eighteenth-century buildings designed by John Wood, which by the nineteenth century had grown into a concert hall and *Grand Pump Room* salon.

A museum now displays artifacts from the Roman occupation and Sulis temple. The great pediment which had crowned the columns of the temple is in pieces in the museum, the face sculpted upon it viewed variously as a Gorgon, a water god, and a sun god. Fragments of Roman mosaic floors survive. The Roman Bath is one story below the street. The pool is filled with green water and surrounded by a columned portico; there is no ceiling. At street level people walk around the perimeter and peer over the edge of a stone railing, while other visitors walk around the pool below the street. From Celtic times to the present the water has been regarded as rich in health benefits, and people still drink spa water in the Pump Room and bathe in it in the spas there.

The driver herded his passengers on board for our next destination: Stonehenge, in Wiltshire on the Salisbury Plain. Primed by the visit to the Roman Baths, I was ready to study ancient mysteries and prehistoric people. We drove through miles of green fields, the grassy plains having been reclaimed from development in the 1920s by the National Trust. Our drive ended in a large parking lot filled with tour buses, where we disembarked to walk toward the stones.

Stonehenge was built over a millennium and a half, from c. 3000 B.C. to c. 1600 B.C. The perimeter consists of a circular ditch and embankment believed to be the origin of the site; post-holes, however, provide evidence of communal activity as long ago as 8000 B.C. A queue of tourists walked along the path, contemplating the stones and taking photos. The stones are roped off now, access allowed only by permit and on days sacred to some faiths. It was a self-guided tour, brochures providing landmark maps. I was drawn to this ancient arrangement of stones that offer more questions than answers. There are erect rectangular stones with others laid horizontally on top of them—hard gray stones contrasting with bright, soft green grass and white sky, the land level, and nothing competing with the stones on the horizon. The only thing there is to look at on a plain canvas, the stones demand contemplation.

Stonehenge consists of an outer circle of thirty sarsen stones (vertical) with lintels (horizontal) laid across the tops of the sarsen stones and fitted with tongue-and-groove joints such as used in furniture-making, and an inner circle. The outer circle is one hundred eight feet in diameter, each stone about thirteen feet high and seven feet wide, weighing about two tons. The bluestones of the inner circle were most likely quarried from Wales, perhaps rolled over logs the great distance from there to Wiltshire. Mounds at the north and south points of the circle are called *barrows*. The Avenue is an entrance in the ditch-and-bank circle (in an aerial view The Avenue resembles the handle on a round skillet), and it is aligned with Summer Solstice sunrise and Winter Solstice sunset. Archaeologists have identified a number of holes, some of which contained stones at some distant time, indicative of a greater stone complex in history than what remains now. Aubrey's Holes are named after John Aubrey, who in the seventeenth century began to map and catalog these holes, fifty-six altogether.

Obviously, the stone circle had some astronomical function, but we do not know exactly what that function was. Anthropology suggests that early cultures engaged in nature worship, but we have conjectures only, no hard evidence, for the builders left no written records—other than drawings of a dagger and axe chiseled into four sarsen stones. Evidence of prehistoric cremations suggest Stonehenge was a burial site (there are sixty-four cremations sites for about 150 people in total), and evidence of animal remains in the area suggests that groups of thousands of people gathered together and slaughtered animals at the site for food, or for some other purpose such as ritual sacrifice. Like the Roman Baths, Stonehenge fell into disrepair at times, and the stones had to be re-erected at different periods.

As the line of people advanced around the stone circle path and gazed at the arrangement, most were probably wondering why people built, expanded, repaired, and rebuilt this massive stone circle that aligns with positions of the sun in the heavens, over a period of about fourteen hundred years. Arthurian legends link Merlin and magic and temporal power to Stonehenge; later folk tales added the element of the devil using Merlin to haul the stones. Aubrey believed Stonehenge was a site of ancient Druidic worship. Neo-Pagans and Neo-Druids hold also that the stone circle served a religious purpose, and they have adopted the site for their current religious observances. Some people give extra-terrestrial intelligence credit for the construction of Stonehenge, citing the mystery surrounding the construction techniques and astronomical functions. The fact remains that we do not know why they built Stonehenge, not can we be sure that by reasoning from our own purposes in building edifices great and small that we can shed light on the reasons people constructed Stonehenge 5,000 years ago. But we do know that we are connected to them by the fact that we are builders, and they were builders.

Humans have a desperate need to identify meaning in our individual lives and in our universe. Is our construction of meaning simply *more building*? When the human species builds it imposes order. *Building* contains, compartmentalizes, and assigns functions and roles to physical structures and social and psychological structures, as well (i.e. a throne room is a place to demonstrate allegiance to a leader).

The ancient Celts and the Romans saw the divine in warm springs bubbling up from the earth—the goddess Sulis, for whom they built a temple over the spring. Did the prehistoric people who erected Stonehenge strive to create meaning, too? The drive to create meaning is the endeavor which connects us to them, for we share the same need to make order out of chaos in nature and in human relationships. Yet, although the fascination of Stonehenge may be our human need to create meaning, all the stone circle yields is Mystery.

NEW WORLD MACABRE

America's Stonehenge

S alem, New Hampshire is a stone's throw from Salem, Massachusetts. One day during our Salem, Massachusetts vacation my traveling companion and I took a drive to New Hampshire and visited Bretton Woods and on our return trip, Salem, New Hampshire, to have a look at the mysterious stone formations called Stonehenge on the North American continent.

We spent a wonderful day in New Hampshire, driving northward through thick primeval forest, the roads becoming narrower as we motored farther north, the mountains coming closer, and towns becoming sparser. Sparkling streams of clear blue water running down from the White Mountains bounded the road. The leaves on all sides were golden brown, orange, and yellow. Road signs warned "Brake for Moose. It could Save Your Life. Hundreds of Collisions." It was a sunny October day, temperatures in the high forties.

We drove up the snow-capped Mount Washington, the highest mountain on the east coast of the United States, and traveled from autumn into winter as well. As we climbed the mountain to Bretton Woods, New Hampshire the road became lightly covered with snow, leaves on the roadside no longer visible under their white coating. As we continued upward, snow was falling, several inches already accumulated on the ground, and the temperature had dropped into the thirties.

At the station of the Mt. Washington Cog Railroad we found eighteen inches of snow on the ground, and I changed from shoes into snow boots, donning earmuffs and gloves, as well, for the temperature was now in the twenties and the wind was blowing hard.

The team at the observatory on the mountain's peak has nicknamed Mt. Washington the place with "the worst weather in the world." Before the Depression it had been the location of a resort for the wealthy and elite, trains going up and down the mountain all day.

We purchased tickets for the ride up Mt. Washington, the 152-year-old railroad taking passengers only half-way up the mountain that day, on account of the weather conditions. Sometimes they run steam trains, but today they used a diesel engine. There was no electricity in the visitors' center, power out because of the snowstorm, but they were running on backup generator power.

We chugged up the mountain in cars over fifty years old, the temperature within them in the forties, and we could see our breaths. The tracks were hardly visible, rows of metal barely revealing themselves from under a blanket of snow. Our trip was to be about ninety minutes. The skies were dark with storm clouds, the landscape all white, green pines peaking from their winter coats. We passed a man, his head and hands protruding from the snow covering the rest of him, waving and hollering. We thought he was clowning around, until the train stopped and crew got off with their shovels to unbury him. He had been clearing the snow off the tracks and had fallen into a drift from which he had not been able to extricate himself. The event was considered business as usual by the crew. The train ride up the snow-covered mountain was a fantastic experience.

We returned down the mountain, and the season changed again, autumn taking over from winter. We drove southward through woodlands, small towns appearing on the exit signs along the road slightly more frequently, as we approached Salem, New Hampshire and America's Stonehenge deep in the forest of New England.

The sign at the entrance to America's Stonehenge states that "Both radio-carbon dating (C-14) and the astronomically oriented standing stones indicate the site was constructed at least 4,000 years ago like the Stonehenge of England." We purchased a self-guided tour map and entered the thirty-acre park. The nature trail took us to the site at which 2,000-year-old artifacts had been uncovered: an ancient wigwam and cooling rack; a re-created dug-out canoe, wigwam frame, and cooling rack are on display at the site now. The guide map points out a standing stone resembling a turtle, which it notes was once sacred to early American people. The trail continues on the Double Walled Pathway past the Watch House (a boulder thought to have been used as the wall of a building that once stood there) to the Winter Solstice Monolith, named so because of its alignment with the annual astronomical event.

Sites are marked for a partially-excavated clay deposit and fire pit indicative of pottery manufacture, a sump pit, as well as remains of other structures erected at various times over the last two centuries. The Oracle Chamber consists of Speaking Tube, Roof Opening, Seat, and Closet. The speaking tube may have had an Oz-like purpose in the projection of a disembodied voice. Here is a Running Deer Carving discovered in the 1930s. The Astronomical Viewing Platform was built in 1975 to enable visitors to view the manner in which the stones are placed for astronomical purposes. The Sacrificial Table is a large stone of over four tons, above the speaking tube, named by William Goodwin, who credited the Ancient Celts with having constructed the American Stonehenge; Goodwin is the author of *The Ruins of Great Ireland and New England*. The map marks places changes were made by excavators, vandals, and carbon-daters, as well as constructions Neolithic and post-colonial.

Largely considered a hoax actually fabricated by its owner William Goodwin in the 1930s, still some believe the ruined walls and chambers are the remnants of early Native American construction or Celtic explorers from across the Atlantic. The structures have an astronomical alignment, whoever arranged them that way. Quarrying on the property, and Goodwin's relocations of stones to what he felt were the locations they had been in before being moved in relatively recent times, render accurate archaeological investigation difficult.

America's Stonehenge has inspired television documentaries and has been linked to H. P. Lovecraft. It is a mysterious collection of stones in a forest of the northeastern United States. At worst, it is a pleasant hike along wooded paths and a scavenger hunt to locate the sites on the map; at best, it is an exercise in considering what *was* there before, and who, and what has happened to them. When driving around New England, Salem, New Hampshire is a curious byway, worth a few hours' detour from the trodden path.

Salem Past and Present Intermixt

Uisiting Salem, Massachusetts is an experience at once heart-rending and rousing. Exemplary for owning the sins of its past, now it is (in my opinion, at least) the human rights capital of the world. Contemporary Salem leadership vigorously champions inclusiveness, and the Salem Award Foundation honors people who work for justice in our time. Once infamous for crimes against its own—neighbor accusing neighbor of witchcraft and consorting with the devil—Salem today is "Witch City," with an official Witch (Laurie Cabot); even the police cars bear the logo of a picture of a witch riding a broomstick on their doors. Half a century ago the need for present action had been brought to Salem's attention: although New England has always valued its past, it was the publication of Arthur Miller's *The Crucible* that provided the jolt that restarted the heart of Salem. The parallels drawn by Miller between the Salem Witch Hunt and the current Senator McCarthy *witch hunt* for communists made the people of Salem realize that Americans had failed to learn the lessons of history.

Salem Past

In 1692 Calvinist Massachusetts had been a place where everyone heard of damnation, hellfire, and brimstone—in fact, they heard of Hell morning, noon, and night. Hell, Reverend Parris would exhort his congregation, was for *other* people—Puritans were saved by election. Abigail and Betty (Parris's niece and daughter) were engrossed by his discourses, as were the other children. Puritan

66

children worked and dressed as adults, play was discouraged, sobriety was the order of the day, and Hell provided the only fantasy world the inhabitants of Salem had (in much the same way that social media and role-playing games do in our time).

While at Harvard Theology School, Parris had decided to go to Barbados to make his fortune; failing at that, he came back to the church for his livelihood, but the only living he could find was in the backwaters of Massachusetts, a humiliating comedown. Hopelessness was in the air: the colony was not thriving; people were bickering; Indian raids were increasing during the harsh winter of 1691. Political upheavals in Stuart England resulted in the revocation of the Massachusetts Charter of 1684, and Increase Mather, Ambassador-Extraordinary for the Massachusetts Bay Colony to the English Court, felt that God had forsaken the Puritans and their colony. Furthermore, the Puritans were the most cantankerous, contentious, litigious, and argumentative group of people ever to try to live together. Preoccupied adults weren't paying attention to a group of sixteen-to-twenty-year-old girls, many of them refugees from Indian wars in Maine, who had no outlet for adolescent energy.

Add to the witches' brew, John Indian and Tituba, Reverend Parris's status-symbol slaves, souvenirs of his failed commercial endeavor in the Barbados. When Abigail invited her friends to share the fun she was having listening to Tituba's Barbados lore, the girls were initiated into island magic fortune-telling, fear of consequences serving only to heighten their excitement. Betty started to show signs of catatonia (generally construed as a symptom of the strain of her secret life); then Abigail began staring into space, flapping her arms like a bird, and getting down on all fours and growling. The spells of erratic behavior and convulsions spread among the girls, foremost among whom was Ann Putnam, who would become the ringleader and accuser of Martha Cory. The village doctor, who unsuccessfully tried his physics on the girls, said, "The evil hand is upon them." While some people thought the girls just needed a good whipping, the rest of the villagers were outraged at the idea.

Everyone was becoming excited, and Salem took on a holiday atmosphere. Four years previously, Reverend Cotton Mather, son of Increase Mather, had cleansed a devil out of a family of Boston children and hanged an Irish washerwoman for causing their malady. Everyone had read Mather's report, *Memorable Providences Relating to Witchcraft and Possession*, and some had traveled to Boston for the hanging. Parris proclaimed a state of emergency and called in ministerial reinforcements—crusading devil-routing ministers from Salem Town. "Who is tormenting you?" they asked the girls, and other leading questions. The first to be named—by Betty—was Tituba, along with an old woman tramp, and another old woman who owned land and did not go to church because she was bed-bound. Both women denied the charge. Tituba, however, told them what they wanted to hear about red cats and red rats who said, "Serve me," and had the face of Goody Osborne (the bed-bound old woman). Then Goody Good (the old woman tramp) agreed, and said it was Goody Osborne who was the instigator. Tituba said she tried to resist the tall man's orders to torment the children, but Goody Osborne would force her to obey. This behavior had flared up among adolescent girls from time to time—before as well as after 1692—throughout New England. While today sociologists tend to view the girls' behavior as *normal* responses of women in oppressive societies (much as pacing and repetitive behavior is common to caged animals) the narrative of 1692 was that Satan was waging Armageddon against his arch-enemies, the Puritans.

Fueled by old grudges and jealousies, accusations flew. Arraignments for witchcraft displaced the usual boundary disputes that had filled the court dockets. Thomas Putnam, father of Ann, wrote the testimonies of Ann Putnam and Mercy Lewis and testified against over one hundred witches. The hangings began that summer. As Sarah Good went to the gallows, she cursed Reverend Noyes: "You're a liar! I am no more a witch than you are a wizard! If you take my life away, God will give you blood to drink;" not long after that, he died of a hemorrhage. As the hysteria was spreading like wildfire, the only way a person could elude death was to confess to signing the black man's book, repent (after everything he owned had been confiscated) and then implicate someone else. All who refused were imprisoned. *Spectral evidence* was the most salient feature of the trials: as the accused stood in the box, the girls would have convulsions and point to invisible birds and claim pinches from invisible fingers, all caused, they howled and shrieked, by the witch in the box, and that was sufficient evidence upon which to hang someone. Individual people's stories are piteous. Pious and good folks were hanged, nineteen all together, one man was pressed to death, and others died in prison. Wanting to avoid the start of the judicial process and the confiscation of his property, Giles Cory would not say innocent or guilty, so they laid a board on him and piled stone after stone until he was crushed to death. When asked innocent or guilty, his last words were, "More weight."

Boston ministers had some doubts—not so much about the witchcraft, as about the conduct of the trials. While publicly supporting the trials they simultaneously assisted wealthy people (such as John Alden) to escape. After his wife was accused, Reverend Hale started to have doubts about the whole matter. The madness came to an end when the governor's wife was accused. At least one hundred fifty people had been arrested for witchcraft, and the hysteria was seeping into other Massachusetts towns. By winter Governor Phipps was allowing some of the accused to be released to their families when he knew that the only evidence was spectral evidence. Thanks to Phipps, when trials resumed, they did not admit spectral evidence.

Salem Present

Son of Salem Nathaniel Hawthorne was descended from the Judge Hathorne who had presided over the Witch Trials. Bearing the burden of his family's guilt several generations later, Hawthorne wrote *The Scarlet Letter*, *The House of the Seven Gables* and other novels and short stories that form his condemnation of the great sin of hard-hearted self-righteousness, which he understood to be the root cause of the Witch Trials. Today's Salem has a statue of him on the street near the Hawthorne Hotel. At the nearby actual *House of the Seven Gables* costumed docents tell about Hawthorne's life and works and even enact scenes from the novel of the same name.

The house, built in 1668 by Captain John Turner, has undergone numerous renovations and additions; in homage to the 1851 novel Hester's cent shop was added at a more recent date. Eighteenth-century rooms belonging to the families of the rich Salem sea captains, the Turners and the Ingersolls (Hawthorne's cousins), and a secret staircase are part of the tour of the interior; outside, on the water of Salem Harbor, are Colonial Revival Gardens. Proceeds benefit programs for Salem's immigrants and at-risk youth. Hawthorne's birthplace, erected circa 1750, has been moved to this location.

Noteworthy among Salem landmarks are three cemeteries hallowed by the blood of 1692. The graves of John Hathorne and Bartholemew Gedney (two members of the *Court of Oyer and Terminer* of the Witch Trials) are located in the *Charter Street Burial Point* near the Hawthorne Hotel at the center of Salem. Illuminated by floodlight on October nights, throngs of visitors in Halloween costumes mill among the weathered colonial angel-wing headstones, many leaving flowers on the granite slabs that individually commemorate each of the persons killed during the Witch Trials—their names and their own affecting statements of their innocence are engraved on each stone. The *Howard Street Cemetery* is reached by walking an old narrow alley-like residential street behind the center of town, a tree-shaded street lined with eighteenth and nineteenth-century homes; it was the jail yard in 1692—where Giles Cory was pressed to death—and now is home to people of Salem who have been dead for centuries. *Broad Street*

Cemetery is the final resting place of High Sheriff George Corwin and Judge Jonathan Corwin, on the outskirts of town. Most of the victims were buried in unmarked graves.

The *Witch House*, the oldest original building in Salem and the home of Judge Corwin, is the only building related to the Witch Trials still in existence; visitors can tour the interior and see the lifestyle of wealthy and important personages in the seventeenth-century Massachusetts colony. Outside on the street the interactive drama *Cry Innocent* re-enacts the arrest of Bridget Bishop, after which the multitude follows her to the courthouse where they may purchase tickets to watch her trial unfold—and even participate in seventeenth-century justice.

Salem is a compact, easily walkable town. We enjoy rambling down the narrow brick streets of Salem which are lined with quaint New England bookshops, my favorites being *Wicked Good Books* and *The Marble Faun*. Several stores specialize in occult and Goth accouterments. Eventually we come to a statue of Elizabeth Montgomery (as Samantha Stevens in *Bewitched*, several episodes of which were filmed in Salem) on a square at the other end of town. People—many in Halloween costume and others in witch regalia of long black cloaks and pointed hats—convene here each year from all over the country for the *Witch Parade*. A curious tradition has evolved in tandem with the parade: annually the volume of the music broadcast over the loudspeakers is turned up in order to cover the threats of a man with a bullhorn who comes regularly to tell the merrymakers that they will go to Hell if they do not repent. His placards read: *The Wages of Sin is Death* and *My Father Created Your Mother*. Other signs in the crowd read: *This is How it All Began in 1692* and *Religion: the Biggest Cause of Hatred in the World*. Yet, even so, the atmosphere is not hostile, but festive, a PG-rated *Mardi Gras*-style fete.

While children compete in pumpkin-decorating contests, ride the Ferris wheel on the midway, or watch the magic show at the Hawthorne Hotel, countless programs for adults are underway.

Once the accused witches (none of whom were really witches) had been the victims, but now the Salem community of witches proudly sponsors affairs ranging from serious to festive to celebrate the *Samhain* season—and everyone is invited. At the Hawthorne Hotel one Halloween we attended the *Samhain* Feast (*Samhain* is Celtic for *Halloween*), where an altar on which several skulls were displayed was set apart on the side of the room. Celtic musicians played string and woodwind instruments, and bread was broken together by the participants over dinner. When we had finished eating everyone rose from their tables and stood in the center of the room to form a magic circle that would facilitate our communication with the Dead (Halloween is the traditional harvest-time celebration of death and rebirth when the veil between the worlds is said to be thin).

Black veils and funeral attire are the customary apparel which guests wear to the yearly *Mourning Tea*, a tradition that integrates tea and pastries with ceremonies to honor the Dead. The *Dumb Supper* is a much-anticipated annual formal banquet that commences with mystic rites honoring the Dead. Upon an altar where the Dead are served their dinner before the guests are served theirs, the guests have already placed mementoes of those who have moved on. The courses are served backward—beginning with dessert and ending with salad—and neither the diners nor the wait staff may speak. As people eat their meals in silence, a skull is carried to each person for his or her contemplation—a *memento mori*.

The Witches of Salem offer séances and palm-readings. They also host a broad assortment of magical workshops and macabre programming available to the public. At the *Circle of Stitchery* on the wharf I took part in an intensive introductory Tarot course. (While there I purchased spell kits for keeping safe and for making money.) At the *Charter Street Burial Ground* one chill and starlit October night a witch doctor from New Orleans revealed the secrets of *Graveyard Magic*. I have availed myself of strange opportunities to delve into the weird mysteries of *Necromancy, Scrying into a Dark Mirror, Animal Familiars,* and *Speaking to the Dead with Laurie Cabot* by enrolling in the events sponsored by *Festival of the Dead* and held at the *Omen.*

Seminars and rituals at the *Omen* are conducted in a deeply-red damask wallpapered room lit by black candles whose flickering flames are multiplied in the mirror that rests upon a heavily-carved dark wood sideboard in the late Victorian style. The marble top of the sideboard serves as an altar, on which are arranged crystal balls, human and animal skulls, candles, vials and incense, cauldrons, wands and ceremonial blades. Here *Hekate: Unveiling the Queen of the Dead* began with a survey of the beliefs surrounding the ancient goddess of death—her attributes, her powers, and her symbols—which have undergone a number of permutations across cultures and through the ages. The witches invoked Hekate through a ritual that incorporated dance, chanting, and prayer. One of the witches wore a white veil of gossamer gauze that streamed from a half-mask of silver thistles that concealed her eyes and crowned her head. She wore a floor-length black gown and carried a candle, the picture of an ancient otherworldly being. Another witch in a long black dress, the sleeveless arms of which revealed her extensively tattooed shoulders, wore a black headdress with a skull motif resting on her forehead; a green snake writhed affectionately around her neck. The third enchantress, also in a long black dress, wore a black lace headdress and veil and carried a candle. Next to her a raven perched upon its cage (the witches informed concerned participants that the animals were rescues). By invoking Hekate, those assembled worked to make contact with deceased loved ones. The audience at these events is a mixture of practitioners of *The Craft* and curious tourists.

Historic New England sponsors *Classic Poems for All Hallows Eve* at the seventeenth-century, brown-shingled *Gedney House.* Local poets, actors and writers read poetry with Halloween themes, a sort of *very cold* coffee house (the *Gedney House* is unheated and has no plumbing). The inside walls are stripped of their drywall, the bricks and wood beams of the 1600s laid bare so that architects and archaeologists can study the materials and building techniques of the colonial period. (The house is also spookier that way.) Readings range from Hawthorne's *Doctor Heidegger's Experiment* to Ann Bradstreet's *Upon the Burning of Our House* and Poe's *The Raven*, as well as selections from contemporary writers. This literary gathering is yet one more example of the fluidity of time in Salem, of the merging of past and present.

The costume balls of Salem are renowned with good reason. We have been to the Witches' Ball (whose theme was *Dance of the Tarot*) and the Hawthorne Hotel Ball (whose theme was *A Night to Dismember*). The Hawthorne Hotel fills to capacity with incredible costumes for a very competitive costume contest. Music, dancing, hors d'ouevres, and spirits flow freely in the merry company. Additional costume parties are held at several restaurants; themes in past years have been vampires and steampunk.

A number of the historic houses of Salem are now museums. Additional aspects of Salem history are illuminated by the several Witch Trial museums, the *New England Pirate Museum*, and the *National Park Service Visitors Center*. At *Count Orlok's Nightmare Gallery* (a movie monster museum on the wharf at Salem Harbor) we met Butch Patrick, the grown-up *Eddie Munster*. The *Peabody Essex Museum* (an art museum dedicated to the period before the War of 1812 when Salem was the richest seaport in America) contains stunning eighteenth-century furnishings and decorative arts and an exquisite collection of chinoiserie—it even includes an entire two hundred-year-old Chinese house. The *Peabody-Essex* recently housed a special exhibit of *Metallica's* Kirk Hammet's movie monster props and memorabilia collection, which included his guitars painted with Universal movie monsters and the mask from *The Creature from the Black Lagoon*.

A stupendous array of macabre delights is available in Salem throughout October: over the years we have enjoyed a superb production of *Dracula's Guest* by the Salem Theater Company, a lecture by a Harvard professor on *Dracula* at the *Salem Athenaeum*, and a Salem State University largely-nude performance of *The Master and Margarita*. *Mahi Mahi Harbor Cruises* offers ghost-story tours of the Salem harbor; and the tall ship *Friendship* is docked across from the *Customs House*, at which Nathaniel Hawthorne worked his day job (his desk is still there). Thousands of people in costume couture promenade the narrow streets and take pictures of each other. Speaking of couture—without a pentacle in Salem as I feel as naked as I do without a scarf in Paris, and these are available in all the occult stores, where I love to stock up on Tarot cards, crystal balls, Ouija boards, herbs, and Voodoo dolls. On our 2012 journey to Salem we drove smack into Hurricane Sandy and had a front-row seat as Mother Nature, or the Goddess, if you prefer, demonstrated her power. A comprehensive schedule of all the events in Salem and nearby localities is available at a central website, HauntedHappenings.com. (Hurricane Sandy was *not* on the schedule.)

Hallowmas

The *Hallowmas Feast* was held in *The Cauldron Black*, an occult shop in Salem, Massachusetts, on the wharf in Salem Harbor. It is a close space with black walls and a sound system playing chanting New Age music, an emporium selling shirts, hoodies, and other garments black and screen-printed with white occult symbols. The ware also includes wands, candles, boxes with many compartments, jewelry with pentacles and powers (crystals, pewters), books on various forms of witchcraft, incense and burners, poppets, many Egyptian figures, and oils.

The *Hallowmas Feast* began with participants processing into the inner room, the doorway of which is hung with black cloth serving as a veil between the worlds. The walls of the back room are painted black and hung with images of people dressed in modern occult (Goth) styles. Among both painted people on the walls and live participants, black was the overall fashion choice, accessorized with pewter jewelry, and icons of chalices and snakes and wands. The altar toward which the participants processed was draped in a black lace shawl, long fringes hanging over the table. Beneath the table candlelight flickered through the fringe. A skull, a wand, candles, powders, and other occult paraphernalia were arranged on the altar. Curious signs of obviously occult symbols, whose meaning were an enigma to me, were chalked or painted white on the black wood plank floor in front of the altar. A round table before the altar held a black iron cauldron.

A black-robed man in his late twenties or early thirties with kohl-bordered eyes, his light brown hair close-cut in front, and

grown longer in back and tied into a Japanese-style top-knot, traced
a circle with a bone (most likely an human ulna) on the skin of
a drum, creating a whishing sound. Then he began *Drumming
up the Dead*—those who were ancestors of our blood, bone, and
spirit. As we observe the death of nature and approach of winter,
All Hallows Eve is a time to reflect on our own mortality as well.

The Wizard paid homage to the spirits and to the ancestors.
He invoked first the blameless victims of the Salem witch hunt
of 1692 and then the ancestors of *The Craft* (whom he called "The
Mighty Dead"), and as he spoke he poured a large pinch of salt into
a cauldron. As he repeated the same invocations several times, the
Wizard added water, oil, and incense to the flames, as he worked
to create a sacred space. Next, he picked up a white rose, removed
several petals from it, and dropped the petals into a clear bowl of
water, which he then stirred with the flower from which he had
taken the petals—*Offerings to the Gede Lwa*. The Wizard then
walked down the aisle between the rows of folding chairs, carrying
before him the smoking incense (frankincense and myrrh), as the
congregation waved their hands, gently wafting the smoke toward
their own faces, as they inhaled the perfumed smoke.

Dancing with Death was next on the program. Two dancers
performed—one at a time, not together. They were dressed in
long black dresses, and they had scarves draped over their arms.
They moved in Hindu-style movements, waving their arms and
stretching their bodies before the altar, in time with the drumming.
They were performing for the spirits.

Next, in *Giving Voice to the Dead*, a man led forward a blind seer,
a tall, lithe woman, dressed in an ethereal white Grecian-style toga.
She wore a paper mask on the top part of her face, a mask which
seemed to be the top part of her face, but which covered her eyes (a
trompe l'oeil). With a lovely voice, she sang a song about a flowing
river, that we should follow.

Returning to the altar, the Wizard Justice performed a rite in
preparation for breaking bread and wine in communion with the

dead, and with the participants' own mortality. One of the dancers, a tall, slender woman with black hair, wearing a long black gown took her place at one side of the altar. Across the altar from her was the Wizard. Each held a crescent-shaped knife, the blade up. They overlapped their blades above the altar. The woman held forth in her other hand the chalice of wine. The man held the bread in his. Communicants were instructed to break off a piece of bread, to touch their hands to skull on the altar, and to then touch their own foreheads. Partakers came forward in a line to receive the emblematic foods. Some drank the wine from the chalice, and some dipped their bread in the wine before eating it. Some knelt to receive the communion, and some received it standing.

After the ceremony concluded, everyone processed out from the inner room. The Wizard encouraged them to inhale the smoke in the doorway to cleanse excess energies they did not wish to carry with them, and to splash themselves with the bowl of rose water an altar attendant held in the doorway for them. They were invited to remain in the shop for a little while, to socialize or shop, or just to take some time to return to the mortal world from the spiritual realm in which they had been tarrying. Time was limited, though, for soon the shop was locked up and everyone was hurrying out to join the *Nu Aeon* (Temple of Nine Wells) candlelit procession from the Salem Wharf to *Gallows Hill*, where the victims of the 1692 Witch Hysteria in Salem had been hanged.

Across town, other people were gathering for *The Witches Magic Circle* in the Salem Commons. Thousands of people were creating concentric circles around the witches in the center who were leading the Samhain ceremony. The witches invoked the spirits of the four cardinal directions, and as they called upon each directional spirit they turned to face that way, and so did the people in the circles. The assemblage wore all manner of witch ensembles and Halloween costumes; they were of all ages, from children to the elderly. The presiding witches besought fellowship with each other, and with those who have preceded us in death, for Samhain is the day when the veil between the worlds is the thinnest. The people in the circles danced with the witches, in a stomping, aboriginal step, to the beat of the *Dragon Ritual Drummers*, as the ceremony was completed. When darkness descended people began to disperse and a dance band started to jam on the stage on the other side of the Commons. Fireworks would bring to an end this celebration of Halloween 2018 in Salem.

Ground Zero

S alem Village was born of strife in 1672. The prosperous mercantile townsfolk and the struggling farmers of Salem Town had not been getting along. The farming folk were clamoring for separation from the governance of Salem, and also from the town congregation (for, in addition to their quarrelling, the journey from the village to the town meeting house was arduous, especially in winter). The feisty and argumentative separatists of Salem Village were, lamentably, unaware that they were about to break open Pandora's Box. In 1689, after having formed their separate Church of Christ in Salem Village, the villagers appointed as their minister *Samuel Parris*—and that was the beginning of the end of the Puritan vision:

...we shall find that the God of Israel is among us, when ten of us shall be able to resist a thousand of our enemies, when he shall make us a praise and glory, that men shall say of succeeding plantations: the Lord make us like that of New England: for we must consider that we shall be as a City upon a hill, the eyes of all people are upon us; so that if we deal falsely with our God in this work we have undertaken and to cause him to withdraw his present help from us, we shall be made a story and a by-word through the world, we shall open the mouths of enemies to speak evil of the ways of God, and all professors for God's sake.

Thus prophetically spake John Winthrop, first Governor of Massachusetts in *The Model of Christian Charity* (1630).

Today the place once known as Salem Village is Danvers, Massachusetts, five miles from the present town of Salem. The foundation of the 1681 Parsonage of the Reverend Samuel Parris is here. Although ministers did not typically own their parish homes, Parris was adept at applying pressure to his congregation, and he acquired the deed to his Parsonage by repeated applications of mental coercion. Having been planted, the seed of rancor grew rapidly, for the Reverend was as confrontational as his flock who had separated from their Puritan fellows. He harangued them from the pulpit about his salary and the provision of his firewood. He exhorted parishioners to fear damnation should they fail to fulfill their obligations to *him*.

In 1692 the witchcraft delusions originated in Salem Village—in the kitchen of the Parsonage—where the slave Tituba was demonstrating to Parris's daughter and niece and their friends how to divine who their future husbands would be. In the Parsonage kitchen the girls learned to think on their feet, to concoct a convincing story—to shift the blame and deflect the consequences of dabbling in island magic in the Parsonage. In order to avoid punishment they lit a conflagration that would end in the death of their neighbors, and they became fiends.

The Parsonage—Ground Zero—is now an archaeological excavation site. Whenever I visit I venture down into Tituba's kitchen with a sense of foreboding—when I place my foot on the dirt and pebble floor that is surrounded by foundation stones—old rounded rocks from the colonial period, not bricks and mortar or concrete—I experience an ominous feeling. The hostility is fresh—not four centuries old. The foundation of the Parsonage bears witness to the malice within the human heart. The Parsonage site is reached by means of an easement through the backyards of some houses in the picturesque town of Danvers. I wonder whether construction on this land was a good thing, whether it carries the risk of contamination, similar to building on a toxic waste site.

On Hobart Street in Danvers is the *Witchcraft Victims Memorial*. Engraved on the front of its large granite central altar are the words:

*In memory of those innocents who died during the Salem
Village Witchcraft Hysteria of 1692.*

Upright granite slabs bear the names of those who died as a
result of the Witch Trials, the names of the victims grouped accord-
ing to the dates they were hanged or otherwise perished:
Hanged August 19, 1692
Rev. GEORGE BURROUGHS of Wells, Maine
Formerly of Salem Village

and

Died in jail March 10, 1693
LYDIA DASTIN of Reading

On top of the granite altar is a granite book on a granite lectern.
The open pages of the book are engraved *The Book of Life*. From
the right and the left sides of the lectern extend chains—chains
which terminate in manacles.

Danvers signs hallow the locations of former Witch Trial sites.
One sign reads:

*The Church in Salem Village: To this church, rent by the
Witchcraft Frenzy, came in 1697 the Reverend Joseph Green,
aged twenty-two. He induced the mischief makers to confess, rec-
onciled the factions, established the first public school, and became
noted for his skill at hunting game and his generous hospitality.*

At the *Witchcraft Victims Memorial* is another sign indicative
of the solemnity with which Danvers accepts its stewardship of
history:

*1672 Salem Village Meeting House: Directly across from
this site was located the original Salem Village Meeting House*

82

where civil and military meetings were held, and ministers,
including George Burroughs, Deodat Lawson, and Samuel
Parris preached. The infamous 1692 Witchcraft Hysteria began
in this neighborhood. On March 1 accused witches Sarah Good,
Sarah Osborn, and Tituba were interrogated in the meeting
house amidst the horrific fits of the "afflicted ones." Thereaf-
ter, numerous others were examined, including Martha Cory,
Rebecca Nurse, Bridget Bishop, Giles Cory, and Mary Esty.
Many dire, as well as heroic deeds transpired in the meeting house.
In 1702 the meeting house was abandoned, dismantled
and removed to this site until the lumber "decayed and became
mixed with the soil."
In 1992 a memorial was erected here to honor the Witchcraft
Victims, and to remind us that we must forever confront intoler-
ance and "witch-hunts" with integrity, clear vision, and courage.

The *Rebecca Nurse Homestead* is in Danvers, too, a large red frame building with additions that have been tacked on here and there by different generations. Originally constructed in 1636 by Townsend Bishop, in 1692 Francis and Rebecca Nurse lived here. Rebecca Nurse was a pious and good woman, known for helping sick people, neighbors in need, and women requiring midwifery assistance. In 1692, seventy-one years old and ill, she was pulled from her sickbed to stand trial as a witch. Nurse is one of the martyrs who refused to plead guilty. No one who pled guilty and named others was executed, just those who maintained their innocence until the end. Nurse believed that to utter so monstrous a lie would imperil her immortal soul, which was dearer to her than her life. So obvious was it to the townspeople that she was a godly woman that Nurse was acquitted of the charge of witchcraft at her first trial—but political forces prevailed and she was found guilty when re-tried. She was hanged in 1692. Behind her house is a cemetery containing a monument to the martyrs of 1692, a poem by John Greenleaf Whittier engraved upon it. Nurse and the Reverend

George Jacobs are buried here. Their families had to retrieve their bodies under cover of darkness because they were forbidden to have custody of them. Some victims' bodies were never located in their unmarked graves.

The large barn-like brown building on the grounds is a reproduction of the Salem Village Meeting House, which had been used for the movie *Three Sovereigns for Sarah* and was afterward relocated to this site. A visitor sitting on a bench and looking up at the pulpit, or very high up at the rafters, can imagine the girls calling out that they were being attacked by invisible birds which had been sent (they cried) by the accused person standing in the witness box. Sorrow can weigh intensely if one envisions the *afflicted girls* writhing in contractions—and blaming their bewildered neighbors for bewitching them.

The *Putnam House* is in Danvers, as well. Built in 1648, it was home to Ann Putnam's uncle Joseph. Everyone was in danger of becoming the next accused—particularly those who, like Joseph, decried the grisly proceedings. Joseph kept his guns and horses ready so that he could flee at a moment's notice were he to be accused. Also still extant in Danvers is the home of Sarah Holten, who testified against Rebecca Nurse. Today the home is known as the *Samuel Holten House*. Built in 1670, it was also home to Samuel Holten, who was a member of the Continental Congress and a hero of the Revolutionary War. The Daughters of the American Revolution owns the Putnam and Holten houses.

In 1752 Danvers made the move to separate itself entirely from Salem, and in 1757 it became a township. It is generally thought that the citizens wished, by changing the name of the town, to disassociate themselves from the notoriety of the bloodbath of 1692. Today Danvers is an agreeable town, with a number of good restaurants and a warm New England feeling. Small streets are filled with Cape Cod houses and autumn leaves partially cover old colonial period stone walls. As we drive around the narrow, winding streets blanketed by leaves of yellow and gold, visiting the relics of the sorrowful time, I find myself reflecting on all the people who have traveled these roads over the centuries, and I consider all the lives that have been lived in this place through which I am passing now. And on my skin I feel the residue of the griefs of 1692.

The Boston Thread

While sojourning in Salem, my friend and I like to make excursions to other beguiling destinations, of which New England has no shortage. From Salem it is any easy drive to Concord, the home of Louisa May Alcott and the *Sleepy Hollow Cemetery* (the resting places of Alcott, Hawthorne, and Thoreau); and Salem is not far from the *Plimoth Plantation* (where the Pilgrims came to the Americas in 1620). By ferry Boston is only a short jaunt from Salem, too. (Riding the ferry requires half the time and none of the forbearance needed when taking on the Boston-area freeways; not having to find a city parking space is an added windfall.)

On our last trip from Salem to Boston we visited the *Boston Tea Party Museum*. Here interactive programs assign roles to visitors, some of whom are given lines to speak aloud, as they enter the colonists' debate regarding the best policy for addressing the propensity of the English Crown to add new taxes without granting the colonists the benefits of representation. Costumed docents next guide visitors to a chamber where hologram colonists are engaged in a heated discussion—in the course of which dividing themselves into patriots and loyalists. Then the visitors board a ship in the Boston Harbor and throw parcels of tea overboard into the water, as they did in 1773 (the "tea" is on a tether, so that it can be pulled back on board to allow everyone a turn).

Generally we walk the *Boston Freedom Trail*. Sixteen historic places that attest to the American struggle for Freedom are linked by a two-and-a-half mile trail of painted bricks through the city. The modern city has grown up around the historical sites where

Freedom was strived for by people who held the great ideal of a nation "of the people, by the people, and for the people." The *Freedom Trail* begins in the Boston Commons and proceeds to the *Massachusetts State House* and *Park Street Church*, thence to the *Granary Burying Ground*. The burying ground, founded in 1660, features weather-erased colonial skulls with angel wings and topsy-turvy headstones. Freedom fighters are buried here: Paul Revere, Sam Adams, John Hancock, Robert Paine, and the victims of the Boston Massacre. Here also are the remains which once were Samuel Sewell, Salem Witch Trials judge (who seems out of place among the fathers of our liberty). The Puritans of Boston would share none of their land for the construction of the Anglican church ordered by King James, so the Crown claimed part of the cemetery (now called the *King's Chapel Burying Ground*) to erect the *King James Chapel* upon it, which is the next stop on the *Freedom Trail*. In the *King's Chapel Burying Ground* are buried Mary Chilton (the first Pilgrim to step onto Plymouth Rock) and John Winthrop (the first governor of Massachusetts). A statue of Benjamin Franklin marks the next stop, the site of the *Boston Latin School*, whose alumni include patriots Sam Adams and Ben Franklin—and Cotton Mather.

Anne Hutchinson—banished from the Puritan Plantation of Massachusetts for the nonconformity of her conscience—once lived at the site of the next stop on the *Freedom Trail*, *The Old Corner Bookstore*. It was here that *The Scarlet Letter* and *The Battle Hymn of the Republic* were published. Nathaniel Hawthorne and Charles Dickens hung out here with the literati of a young America. The *Freedom Trail* wends its way past the *Old South Meeting House*, the *Old State House*, and the site of the *Boston Massacre* to *Faneuil Hall*, an early American marketplace that continues the tradition with a cornucopia of restaurants and shops.

The trail stops next at the grey gabled colonial house, where from 1770 until 1800 Paul Revere lived. This house had been built in 1680 upon the site of the former parsonage of the *Second Church of*

Boston, which had been the home of Increase and Cotton Mather. (It had burned down in 1676.)

From there, the brick trail takes us to the next stop in the story of the struggle for American Freedom—*The Old North Church*. Paul Revere's statue stands before the church. A wrought iron fence surrounds the church whose tall white steeple rises high above the trees. Two lanterns were hung in that steeple "on the eighteenth of April in seventy-five"—as Henry Wadsworth Longfellow has engraved upon the collective American memory—when Paul Revere and the patriots spread the alarm hours before the Battles of Lexington and Concord, when the United States was born. The *Old North Church*, an active Episcopal church now, offers tours of the interior, wherein eighteenth-century brass chandeliers shed light upon white wooden box pews, and large windows of plate glass allow the sun to fill the church.

The final sites on the *Freedom Trail* are the *U.S.S. Constitution* (a.k.a. "Old Ironsides" of the War of 1812) and the obelisk of the *Bunker Hill Monument*. Prior to reaching these last two sites, though, we come to *Copp's Hill Burying Ground*. Here we have visited the graves of Increase and Cotton Mather.

Even granting the fact that the Massachusetts Bay Colony had been established by the Puritans, still it does seem ironic that the Mathers' names are so often found among the footnotes of the *Boston Freedom Trail* histories. The irony is that the sites along the *Freedom Trail* are consecrated to the American cause of liberty. The Puritan theocrats, however—the Mather father and son most prominent among them– during their watch strove mercilessly to deny the people of Massachusetts the liberty of their own consciences. Their ruthless, unyielding, and dogmatic approach to the shepherding of their flock caused people to die. And it brought about the miserable failure of their own religious enterprise in the New World.

Standing upon their graves, I thus denounced the stony hearts of the Mather father and son, who had stoked the flames of the Witch Hysteria.

A black cat appeared on their grave as we turned to leave. As she made her stately progress from one end of the cemetery to the other, she paused occasionally to groom herself or cast a sidelong glance at the people in the graveyard, resisting calls of, "Here, Kitty." What followed afterward bespeaks the power of witchcraft! As we were trying to make the simple journey through Boston traffic to our hotel in Andover, which should have been half an hour, we repeatedly found ourselves lost and hindered by detours, and the trek stretched into three hours. Once more that self-same night, after we had enjoyed a conjuring program at the *Omen* in Salem, malevolent forces prevailed—when we tried to return to our hotel in Andover and a twenty-minute drive mysteriously developed into a ninety-minute nightmare—and we missed our exit and were ticketed for backing up on the berm and then somehow ended up in New Hampshire! Doubt ye not that the wicked and malicious legacy of the Mathers still survives to visit evil upon their fellow men! How else can our difficulties as travelers be explained, other than that there be witches among us?

Lizzie Borden Bed and Breakfast

Fall River, Massachusetts is a pleasant day's excursion from Salem on a rainy day. That day it was raining cats and dogs. We were in Salem for a fortnight, and had reserved the Lizzie Borden House for inclement weather, when it was too wet to slosh around Salem streets. The unsolved murders of Lizzie's parents, Andrew and Abby Borden, and the general supposition that Lizzie was the murderess, who got off scot-free, make the Borden home a popular destination for ghost-hunters.

11:10 AM, August 4, 1892, the Borden's maid Bridget was startled by Lizzie's calling to her, "Maggie, come quick! Father's dead. Somebody came in and killed him." It was a stiflingly hot day, and the Borden household were all suffering from dyspepsia. Lizzie and Bridget were the only ones at home at the time. Andrew had been hacked by an axe, on the living room sofa where he had been lying. He was a wealthy man, a mill manager and property developer, but he was also a tightwad; the Bordens had no electricity or indoor plumbing, which were quite common in Fall River. He had been hacked in the head about a dozen times, splitting his eyeball in half. The estimated time of his death was 11:00 AM, the blood still wet.

At the time of the discovery of her father, Lizzie told Bridget that her step-mother had received a note to visit a sick friend, and that she was not home, but when Bridget and neighbor Mrs. Churchill were going up the stairs, they could see Abby's body on the far side of the bed in the guestroom. She had been facing her killer when she was struck, and after she had fallen on her face, she received seventeen more hatchet blows to the back of her head. Andrew had married Abby when Lizzie was five. Theorists suggest that there were hard feelings relative to Andrew's disposal of property to Abby's family; Lizzie and her sister felt that they had been short-changed. They also suggest that dysfunctional relationships provided the motive for Lizzie's double murders—theories include abuse and incest. The family had been suffering from a gastrointestinal illness that week, as well, and the heat was unbearable. It is proposed that the combination of illness and heat brought the smoldering resentments of the murderess to a head.

Lizzie's testimony was full of inconsistencies. She said she had taken off her father's boots and put his slippers on when he came home from work, but police photos show him wearing boots. She said she had been ironing when her father came home, and another time she said that she had been reading. Her composure appalled people—she lacked emotion. Police did only a perfunctory search of the house, and let her remain there during the investigation. She had been observed burning in the stove a dress with a "paint" stain. The investigation became more earnest, but not until two days after the murders.

The district attorney was rather too forceful for public opinion, especially when addressing a lady, daughter of one of the leading men of the community. The heads were removed from both victims' bodies for autopsies, and when the skulls with hatchet wounds were presented as evidence in court, Victorian jurors were shocked. Much of the evidence presented at the inquest was dismissed, including Lizzie's purchase of prussic acid for cleaning the day before. Allowances were made for Lizzie's flat affect and discrepancies in testimony. Lizzie Borden was acquitted.

Lizzie and her sister, Emma, who had not been home the day of the murders, continued to live in Fall River. Although they inherited their father's estate and moved to a comfortable part of the city, Lizzie was ostracized by the community, for many still believed her guilty. In 1905 the sisters had a disagreement, and Emma moved to another home. Both sisters died in 1927.

The Borden home is a three-story green frame building, the front door approached by four steps to the stoop. A fenced-in yard surrounds the house on the quiet street. The house is now a bed and breakfast offering forensics and paranormal tours. Some people in the neighborhood still feel uncomfortable about the property being there.

On that soggy October day in Massachusetts, we made quickly for the door. We entered in the gift shop, where numerous books and DVD's about Lizzie Borden were for sale, as well as "blood-stained" t-shirts, "bloody" rubber hatchets, and refrigerator magnets of the crime scene photos. After purchasing our tickets, we entered the house, where four or five other people were assembled. We waited in the parlor for the tour to start. The room has floral green carpeting and striped floral wallpaper on a yellow background. Red velvet drapery is hung with tassels. The late Victorian furnishings include a wood-framed camelback sofa and marble-topped harp tables; globe lamps were lit on that dark afternoon.

The tour guide walked us through the sequence of events of the fateful day: he pointed out the place where Andrew had been slain, and as we walked up the stairs, he indicated the step from which the body of Abby was first sighted. From that step the bed in the guest room can be seen, and part of her body on the far side of the bed had been visible from the stairs that day. In the guest room, the dress Elizabeth Montgomery wore in the 1975 movie *The Legend of Lizzie Borden* is on display.

In the kitchen we saw the stove in which Lizzie had burnt her stained dress. This kitchen was where the Borden household had had to eat old mutton soup all that long, hot summer, most likely the cause of the digestive discomforts of the family. We were shown the coroner's board on which the bodies had been laid out on the dining room table, and the broken, blood-stained axe. The tour includes the crime scene photos. The guide told us that Mrs.

Borden's dress had been pulled up when she was found, and that for decency's sake they had pulled it down before photographing her prone body on the floor between the dresser and the bed.

Not long after the murders, the famous song I sang as a child was written, but no one knows who the author is:

Lizzie Borden took an axe
And gave her mother forty whacks.
When she saw what she had done
She gave her father forty-one.

Today there are websites devoted to the paranormal activity at the Borden house. Ghost-hunters' investigations there have been featured on many television programs, including *Unsolved Mysteries, Monsterquest, Paranormal Journeys, Ghost Hunters* and the History Channel. Tours are offered every day of the year but Thanksgiving and Christmas. The tour guide reminded us that the house was now a bed and breakfast, and that we could spend the night. He said someone would come in the morning to cook breakfast, but that at night only the guests would be there. "At least you know you'll be staying with other people who like the same things," he said. Was that supposed to be a comforting thought?

Dark Dreams Come True

For half a century one television show has held the number one spot in my line-up—and the line-ups of thousands of other fans of more than one generation. *Dark Shadows* aired on ABC weekday afternoons from 1966 to 1971. Through 1,225 episodes, this gothic soap opera caused millions of fans to hurry home from school or work to follow the stories of governess Victoria Winters and the mysterious Collins family who live in an imposing mansion high atop Widows' Hill.

The family is plagued by vampires, werewolves, witches and ghosts. The plots largely derive from classic horror literature ranging from Greek mythology to Oscar Wilde and H.P. Lovecraft, and they involve time travel and parallel time. In addition to the original series, *Dark Shadows* lives on in three major motion pictures, a 1991 television revival series, and currently in Big Finish Productions audio dramas. *Dark Shadows* is available on DVD's and is streaming.

There is no turning back once you are bitten by the conceit of the gothic Collinwood mansion of Collinsport, Maine—and especially by its resident dark romantic hero, the undead Barnabas Collins. The world of *Dark Shadows* merges with your world—and you enter the cobwebbed corridors of fandom. Carrying your lantern to light the shadowy corners of the closed-off West Wing, you zealously navigate your way through the mysterious secret passages of *Dark Shadows* Festivals.

2014 Dark Shadows Festival

With my *Dark Shadows* friend, I attended two *Dark Shadows* Festivals—2014 and 2016—which were held in Tarrytown, New York. We came in a day early to spend a day in the Big Apple. Our first stop was FAO Schwartz, where I shuffled off to Buffalo on the *Big* piano. Afterwards, I shopped the rarified atmosphere of Bergdorf Goodman and then tried on bracelets at Cartier. We took the ferry to Staten Island.

By the time we returned to Tarrytown, the *Dark Shadows* fans had arrived in force. Hundreds of people were mingling in the lobby of the Doubletree Hilton. Many of them had been attending conventions every year since the 1980s. Generally, conventions would alternate between East and West Coasts from one year to the next.

My friend and I were among the first to arrive at Lyndhurst the next morning, where registration was held for the Festival. Lyndhurst is the mansion used for Collinwood in the MGM movies *House of Dark Shadows* (1970) and *Night of Dark Shadows* (1971). It is a Gilded Age Gothic Revival mansion on the bank of the Hudson River.

This was our first visit to Lyndhurst. The convention began here—with a tour of what we considered the haunted ancestral estate of *our* childhood! My first impression upon passing through the wrought iron front doors to enter the marble foyer was—that little set design had been required for filming a vampire movie here—*Lyndhurst is move-in ready for a vampire.* The tour guide pointed out a crack in the tile of the foyer—*where Mrs. Johnson had dropped a tray when she was startled by a vampire-killed Carolyn Stoddard* in *House of Dark Shadows.* Portraits of vampire Barnabas Collins and Angelique Bouchard—the wench who was a witch that Barnabas spurned—were prominently placed for the pleasure of the fans. We saw the dining room where young David Collins came in to tell his family that he had seen his dead cousin alive again. Everyone *ooh-ed* and *aah-ed* as we climbed the stairs which led to the tower in which Quentin Collins became overly involved with the spirit of the dead Angelique, much to the dismay of his wife Tracy.

Our exploration of Lyndhurst continued outdoors on the estate. I felt I was walking into the movie when I entered the skeletal greenhouse that is missing a lot of glass—which is the site of ghostly attack in *Night of Dark Shadows*. I crept around the dilapidated pool house—where Quentin tried to drown his wife Tracy in the murky water. I saw the bridge overhanging the railroad tracks where Gerard Stiles fought Quentin. I tried to figure out which tree was used to hang Angelique—didn't they know they could not get rid of her that easily? On a little cottage a sign hangs that designates it *Rose Cottage*—that is where the ghosts of Carrie and Tad took possession of the children. I was in a state of exhilaration: I had physically entered my fantasy world.

I returned to the stables and purchased a t-shirt bearing the handsome visages of Barnabas and Quentin, a *Dark Shadows* calendar, and the soundtrack of the TV show on CD's. I then attained one of the high points of my life—I made the rounds of the stars' tables, getting autographs from Lara Parker (Angelique), Kathryn Leigh Scott (Maggie Evans and Josette DuPres), David Selby (Quentin), Marie Wallace (Eve), Christopher Pennock (Jeb Hawkes and Cyrus Longworth), James Storm (Gerard Stiles), and Sharon Smyth (Sarah Collins). The actors signed my program and calendar. When Lara Parker autographed the book I purchased from her—*Angelique's Descent*—in her elegant script I thanked her in all sincerity for making this the happiest day of my life, and she replied, "You've got to be kidding."

But I was not kidding, for I had met Angelique and Josette and Quentin, and I had entered Collinwood. All my life these had peopled my mind, waking and dreaming, so that day was literally a dream come true for me.

In the tent the stars were entertaining their fans. They told backstage stories, performed their own poetry and music, acted skits, and answered fans' questions in a Q&A session. There was no time to eat, lest we miss some programming, so we settled for snacks sold in the stables—a small sacrifice for the exciting experience.

Dark Shadows stars are approachable; they are engaged in making happy memories. At the conclusion of the programming, the *House of Dark Shadows* and *Night of Dark Shadows* movies were screened under the tent. Following the movies, Sharon Smyth spooked her admirers with ghost stories after dark on the lawn surrounding the gazebo at the Doubletree Hotel.

Day Two began with a luncheon at the hotel. The stars sat at the tables among the fans. *Dark Shadows* memorabilia were raffled for charity, and door prizes were given—*Dark Shadows* books and DVD's and Barnabas rings. Stars entertained on stage, reprising old roles and presenting new work.

When the tables had been cleared, I went among the vendors, where I procured *Dark Shadows* characters' drivers licenses—Willie Loomis is a Blood Donor; Angelique's license lists her allergy as Fire; Quentin is allergic to Silver and has a Full Moon restriction on his license. I obtained autographed photos from Kathryn Leigh Scott and Lara Parker. I acquired a script of the *Dark Shadows* episode videotaped July 16, 1967—crews' comments are scrawled all over it. In this episode Julia Hoffman notices that Victoria Winters is being drawn into the past—and the clutches of Barnabas Collins—by her fascination with Josette's music box.

In the afternoon a caravan of fans made their way to Sleepy Hollow Cemetery for a special guided tour for *Dark Shadows Festival* fans. I spied a young man sporting Quentin sideburns. Listed on the National Register of Historic Places, Sleepy Hollow Cemetery is the final resting place of Brooke and Vincent Astor, Andrew Carnegie, and Washington Irving. Graced with sculptures by leading artists of the late nineteenth-century, it is a macabre outdoor museum. The tour guide directed our attention to an collection of Victorian monuments to grief—a sculpted marble girl clinging to a cross, an angel dropping petals on a grave, a woman draped over the name of her dear departed spouse. She led us to the grave of Washington Irving (the author of *The Legend of Sleepy Hollow*) and revealed that his headstone had been replaced, because so many pieces from the original had been hacked off by his fans as to quite destroy it. Out of all the eerie mausoleums, I particularly appreciated the one covered entirely in ivy.

We came at last to the Collins family mausoleum—where Willy let Barnabas out of the chained coffin which had confined him for one hundred seventy-five years—in the process captivating the imaginations of several generations of devotees. For the two MGM movies the name *Collins* had been added above the doorway and additional angel figures affixed to the building. Carolyn's funeral in *House of Dark Shadows* was filmed at this mausoleum—the local fire department provided the pouring rain with their hoses. The guide brought us *into the mausoleum*—and indicated the shelf reserved for Barnabas. It contains his framed photograph and fangs. In winter, when the ground was frozen, bodies were temporarily stored in mausoleums until spring when they could be interred in the earth.

2016 Fiftieth Anniversary Dark Shadows Festival

We returned to Tarrytown in 2016 for the Fiftieth Anniversary of the first airing of *Dark Shadows*. *Dark Shadows* went on the air June 27, 1966.

The afternoon before the celebration we explored Tarrytown. Wearing my *Collinsport, Maine 1972* t-shirt—a promotional item for the 2012 Johnny Depp *Dark Shadows* movie—I posed for a photo outside the Old Dutch Church. We walked along the Hudson River, bathed in the orange of sunset—the orb in the sky a straight line reflected across the rippling dark blue water, the mountains in the background a dark silhouette.

That evening at the hotel the Fiftieth-Anniversary celebration began—with Nancy Barrett (Carolyn Stoddard), Kathryn Leigh Scott, David Selby, Marie Wallace, Christopher Pennock, James Storm, Lara Parker, and Roger Davis (Peter Bradford and Charles Delaware Tate). In the ballroom, fans viewed film clips—an episode of *Dark Shadows*, and a 1968 Dick Cavett interview of Jonathan

Frid (Barnabas Collins), as well as the two *Dark Shadows* movies, and a new movie—*Doctor Mabuse*, starring Kathryn Leigh Scott, Lara Parker, and Jerry Lacey (Reverend Trask). By then it was well after midnight, and I could not handle any more bliss. The party continued after I had turned in.

Saturday we watched hilarious fan videos—parodies and spoofs of characters and plots—followed by a special airing of *The House*. *The House* is an early television drama that predated *Dark Shadows*. It was written by *Dark Shadows* writer Art Wallace and includes many of the characters and elements with which Wallace went on to create *Dark Shadows*.

I was fortunate to win several lots in the charity auction: a photo of Jonathan Frid at Seaview in 1986, a *Quentin's Theme* LP record (which David Selby signed for me), and a cardboard cut-out of Barnabas advertising that *Dark Shadows* was now available on VHS. The waitress uniform, saddle shoes, and hair fall worn by Maggie Evans in the early episodes of *Dark Shadows* were donated by Kathryn Leigh Scott and went to a lucky fan.

This year I bought the coffin-box DVD set of all twelve hundred twenty-five episodes and carried it with me from table to table, obtaining stars' autographs upon the casket. Cast members graciously agreed to photo after photo with their fans. I had mine taken with Nancy Barrett and Marie Wallace. Kathryn Leigh Scott posed with me when she autographed her books—*Dark Shadows: Return to Collinwood* and *Dark Passages*. I had so enjoyed Lara Parker's *Angelique's Descent* that I bought her other *Dark Shadows* books, *Full Moon Rising* and *The Salem Branch*. She autographed them and posed for another photo, telling me that *Heiress of Collinwood* would be out in a couple of months.

The afternoon programming included Fiftieth Anniversary Q&A's, clips of bloopers from the television show, as well as a tribute to producer Dan Curtis—dearly beloved by *Dark Shadows* fans—who had an impressive career in television and on the big screen. Curtis is known for producing, in addition to *Dark Shadows*, *Winds of War*.

I dressed as Angelique for the costume party, in blue evening gown, elbow-length white gloves, and curly blonde wig. My friend came as Barnabas, in a cape and carrying the famous wolf-headed cane. Lara Parker and Kathryn Leigh Scott dressed as Angelique and Josette, and posed with us! Other fans dressed as Buzz and Carolyn and Dr. Julia Hoffman, Magda, and Reverend Trask. We waited in the service corridor while the fan talent show commenced, until they called us to the stage.

I played the part of Angelique, promptly dying upon two chairs put together as a sofa. The part of Barnabas was played by my friend. Angelique had been shot and was dying—and just as she died Barnabas pronounced the words that he had loved her all along. Had he told her that at the beginning, four years of plot revolving around Angelique's anger and revenge would not have been written, and it would have been a different show! We recreated her death scene from the television show.

The late-night entertainment for the hardy were movies featuring *Dark Shadows* cast members: *On a Country Road* and *The Last Case of August T. Harrison*. After *On a Country Road* I had to cede victory to the Sandman.

Sunday, alas, was the final day of the *Dark Shadows* Festival. I enjoyed an early morning walk to the near-by grounds of Lyndhurst, and then returned to the hotel for the Luncheon. Stars were scattered around the ballroom, seated among their guests. At our table sat Roger Davis and two members of the production crew. We received door prizes and gift bags full of *Dark Shadows* loot. An affecting tribute was made to the cast and crew who had passed on. David Selby and Nancy Barrett waltzed and sang *I Wanna Dance with You*, reprising the roles of Quentin and Pansy Faye from the 1897 storyline.

At a second charity auction I won a Jonathan Frid photo signed "To Kathy"—it was as if Barnabas had returned from the dead to give me his autograph. I also obtained *Shadows on the Wall*, the *Dark Shadows* bible. This was a treasure—it is the proposal for the series, written by Art Wallace, and presented to ABC in 1965. The Festival closed once more with a private tour of Sleepy Hollow Cemetery.

In the evening, after the conclusion of the *Dark Shadows Festival*, we traveled by train from Tarrytown to New York City. It was a short ride—and less stressful and expensive than taking a car into the city. We disembarked at the Grand Central Station, still bustling at ten o'clock at night. Quite a few trains were still loading and unloading passengers. We delighted in the majestic marble architecture of the main concourse. After we enjoyed a very late dinner, we walked the still-busy, brightly-lit blocks of Fifth Avenue at midnight. At the Empire State Building there was a man with a guitar and a sign that read, "Give me $1 or I am voting Trump." A bicycle rickshaw took us to Times Square, which was filled with wall-to-wall people well past midnight, the renowned billboards rendering the night brilliant with moving pictures. Incredibly, the stores were still open. Later, we returned to Grand Central Station and boarded the train for Tarrytown.

The afterglow has not diminished. When I look at my photos and reminisce, when I watch my (almost) daily portion of *Dark Shadows*, when I reconnect with *Dark Shadows* friends, the flame revives. It is good to have a fandom, to enjoy a fantasy world.

Halloween in the Hudson River Valley

H alloween in the Hudson Valley—where the holiday (as we know it today) was invented by Brom Bones, who transformed a harvest celebration into a night of terror when he galloped on a midnight black steed carrying his pumpkin head and tossed it at Ichabod Crane. I was driving Route 80, spanning the breadth of Pennsylvania, back into history, to the time when the Dutch first came to the American shores, where they encountered the dark, alluring mystery of the Catskills and the Pocantico Hills where lurked fearsome beasts and terrifying native people whose skin had a reddish cast that scared the paler Europeans. It was not difficult to conjure that world as I drove—the inky black of the night was just yielding to the dawn, and I thought of Washington Irving's Rip Van Winkle awakening from his twenty-year slumber to discover himself in a strange new realm of wonder and enchantment. I spurred my mechanical steed down and up the steep gradients of the Pennsylvania road as the gradually brightening sky revealed that I was driving into a thick grey mist which was rising from the valley too far below to be seen through the fog. A road sign quite unnecessarily declared *Fog Area*. By the time I was driving past the Dubois exit sign the fog was thick and black; yet, I was able to discern the steep rocky cliffs of the Appalachians. Bright orange, red, and yellow-robed fall forests stood an honor guard next to the freeway. As the sky yielded more light I could see huge clouds of mist billowing up from the valley. A sign for *Bald Eagle State Park* was visible in the orange sky. As I entered New York, road signs increasingly featured Dutch names with all their "vons" and oh-so-many "o's". I anticipated with delight the sight of the Tappan Zee Bridge.

The bridge (now known as the *Governor Mario Cuomo Bridge*) spans the Tappan Zee, a three-mile wide spot on the Hudson River that stretches for ten miles along the coasts of Westchester County and adjacent Rockland County. "Tappan" refers to the local tribe of Delaware Indians and "Zee" is the Dutch word for "sea." The cliffs of the Palisades Mountains form the sides of the Tappan Zee basin. The River was named for Henry Hudson, who was hoping that he had come across the mythical Northwest Passage, a short-cut through the American continent to the wealth of the Orient.

I love coming back to some places. The Hudson River Valley (which includes Tarrytown, Sleepy Hollow, and Irvington) is rich in its heritage of ghost tales and macabre lore. Jewel-toned mountains and hills, the old Dutch buildings, and the prevalence of jack-o-lanterns hint of secrets contained in this vale. I had chosen the Doubletree Hotel in Tarrytown for my home this week because it is within easy walking distance of *Lyndhurst*, and because of a sentimental association with *Dark Shadows Festivals*, the last two of which were held there. After settling into my room, I set out for Philipsburg Manor.

Philipsburg Manor is a seventeenth-century mill, house, and barn established by Adolphus Philipse for the raising of cash crops; his water mill ground grains for export. All the myriad processes required between the planting of the grain and the exportation of the flour are described by docents: they explain how the wheat was first dried in the rafters high above the floor of the great barn. In the barn visitors enjoy demonstrations of *threshing*, of the separation of the seeds from the grain—I even gave it a try myself, awkwardly flailing the sticks on a rope (they resemble nunchucks) to pound the wheat. Visitors are shown how flax is made into linen and straw into hats, baskets, and mattresses. None of the grain goes to waste: stone walls are held together with a straw paste; even the remnants of the wheat are used as fire starters. A cat is kept on staff, an orange tabby whose job is mouse patrol to protect the wheat and play with the visitors.

A vegetable garden features jack-o-lantern scarecrows, and an herb garden provides home-grown pharmaceuticals. Adolphus Philipse ran a multinational business, exporting thirty-two thousand pounds of flour each week. Sloops used to carry Philipse's flour from Philipsburg Manor down the Hudson to New York City and thence to the Caribbean; Philipse's boats would bring back sugar and spices. The Philipse family owned 52,000 acres—most of present-day Westchester County; some of the land was farmed by tenant farmers who paid their rent in wheat. The only food produced for consumption on the estate was that which the slaves and tenant farmers grew for themselves. The Philipse family rarely came here (they lived in Manhattan); the twenty-three slaves who worked the plantation and the overseer were the only people who lived at the Manor. Adolphus came here quarterly to check on his manufactory.

Northern slaves, the tour guide explained, were skilled in the trades, rather than in agricultural labor; they were coopers, millers, and wheelwrights. Our tour began in the old stone manor house, which we entered via a room built into the ground (a la *split level*), through the double Dutch doors whose top half could be opened to let in light and fresh air, while the bottom half could be closed to keep children in and animals out. We were taken into the basement dairy where the guide explained the process of churning wooden buckets of milk from the seventeen cows on the estate—carried by yokes on the shoulders of the dairy workers—into fresh butter and cheese every day. The dairy was constructed of brick floors and whitewashed stone walls, a low wood-beamed ceiling above. Barrels (called *firkins*) would have held seventy-two pounds of butter layered with salt packaged for export. Adjacent to the dairy is the kitchen; here, the meals for the twenty-three workers were prepared in a fireplace and served on wooden dishes, and workers slept on bedrolls filled with straw on the floor before the hearth.

According to the docent, the slaves' primary deterrent to running away was that they would have had to leave their families behind.

The house tour above stairs takes visitors through rooms with high ceilings, lead glass windows, and elaborately carved wooden furniture. The pewter dishes on the tables, the containers for the luxuries of tea and chocolate, the coffee grinders, and marzipan molds reveals the wealth of the proprietor. On the second floor are bedrooms with heavily-carved Old World beds covered with exquisitely embroidered curtains and counterpanes, also a display of wigs on stands, a porcelain wash basin and stand, a chamber pot, and a powder horn and belt, as well as a backgammon game. Exiting through the dining room, I glimpsed the lovely Delft pottery, painted cabinets, and cut glass drinkware. Once we were outside, costumed interpreters explained how meats, and seeds were preserved, and how wool was processed. In 1792 the Philipse property was taken by the new government, for the heirs of Adolphus had sided with the British. Eventually the estate was purchased by John D. Rockefeller, and in the 1940s became the *Sleepy Hollow Restoration Project*, now *Historic Hudson Valley*.

I returned to Philipsburg Manor one evening—this time to experience *The Unsilent Picture*, a black-and-white cult movie whose inspiration came from Washington Irving's *The Adventures of the Mysterious Picture*. Filmed in *Van Cortland Manor* (another Dutch colonial property), this bloodcurdling Halloween film is shown annually at the Philipsburg Manor Visitors Center. The movie is silent, except for the non-verbal noises (such as grunts, slurps, and sneezes); the macabre music and acoustic sound effects are produced by a live performer. At the close of a long day of hiking up and down the mountain-side estate of *Kykuit*, settling down to enjoy a macabre tale well-told was a spine-tingling pleasure.

A grand tour of Kykuit originates at the Visitors Center of Philipsburg Manor, where tourists board a shuttle that carries them up into Pocantico Hills. Kykuit is the estate built in 1906 by John D. Rockefeller, founder of Standard Oil, inhabited by four generations of Rockefellers, and then given to the *National Trust for Historic Preservation* in 1979. Despite its being a grand mansion, the house is rather cozy, consisting of relatively small, intimate rooms. Ming Dynasty porcelains grace the music room, which is crowned by an oculus on the ceiling that is encircled by a white gallery rail—the plasterwork on the ceiling is beautiful in its own right. Rooms on the west side of the house have large picture windows for viewing the Hudson River and Palisade Mountains. A portrait of John D. Rockefeller Sr. painted by John Singer Sargent hangs in the dining room, where the table is set with Meissen dinnerware. The china room houses the rest of the dinnerware. Nelson Rockefeller loved modern sculpture, expressionism, and abstract art, and he filled the house and grounds with it; even the basement is a modern art gallery that has Andy Warhol portraits of Nelson and his wife Happy.

The *Rockefeller State Park Nature Preserve* abuts the extensive grounds of Kykuit. Majestic Oceanus, scepter in hand, faces the Hudson River before the main entrance to the house. From the vantage point of the marble bannister of the Oceanus piazza, the visitor may enjoy the magnificent vista of the Palisades, which in late October is a vital natural tapestry woven in shades orange, vermilion, and emerald. The brickwork of the wall drew my attention: it is a superb mosaic of browns and oranges in the Arts and Crafts style and ivy lushly drapes itself in places over the wall, intensifying the textural appeal of the mosaic. Seventy pieces of modern sculpture are outside on the grounds, including "lawn ornaments" by Picasso and Rodin, part of Nelson's collection. A grotto with a waterfall was created of stones imported from Italy. The *Tea House*, a beautiful stone building with great picture windows, is surrounded by formal flower beds symmetrically laid out. The *Temple of Aphrodite* in the *Arcadia Garden* contains a marvelous statue of Venus that is mounted on a turning pedestal attached to a pole which descends into a round room below ground, where Tiffany stalactite lights illuminate the shadows, classical-style theater masks top the ceiling, and Greek columns support the structure. Kykuit's various structures (of which I have described only a small selection) are built into the mountainside, so that one scrambles up and down steep stone and gravel paths to move between them. To enjoy the outdoor art museum, one is also obliged to experience the natural beauty of the Pocantico terrain, as well.

In addition to the fine art and exquisite landscaping of Kykuit, extensive recreational amenities built for the enjoyment of the Rockefeller family are found on the estate. These include a golf course, a *Playhouse* with a basketball court, billiard room, and indoor and outdoor pools, and a *Coach Barn* that has bachelor apartments and guest rooms and contains all the carriages the Rockefellers ever owned, including the limousine Nelson used when he was Governor of New York and a Model T. Ford. Vaseline globes cast a warm glowing light over the rooms of the Coach Barn. An orangery was pointed out to us as the shuttle wound its way down the hill.

Following a splendid day of what was essentially a stimulating mountain-side outdoor gallery hiking tour and cardio workout, I was ready to enjoy a delicious repast at a family-owned Thai restaurant in Sleepy Hollow, across the street from Philipsburg Manor. I dined with haste, though—for with the setting of the sun and the ascent of the moon and stars, my twilight agenda turned to the macabre world of Irving's Sleepy Hollow. First I was to view *The Unsilent Picture*, and then make my way to the *Old Dutch Church* for *The Legend of Irving*.

The Old Dutch Church is a stone building on a hill next to the *Sleepy Hollow Cemetery*, where Washington Irving is resting, at this time teeming with lantern-tour visitors. Built by Adolphus Philipse in 1687, the Old Dutch Church has been in continual use since (except during the Revolution). Many-paned windows are set into thick white walls. Pale golden light is cast by brass candlestick chandeliers appended to the dark brown rafters over the pews and by the brass sconces punctuating the walls. The congregation assembles before a jack-o-lantern preacher who is perched on the raised pulpit that is reached by a winding wood staircase. This is Washington Irving country, the land of the *Headless Horseman*, the source of America's favorite holiday—Halloween.

In the dimly candle-lit ancient space, the sexton welcomes the audience to the *Reformed Dutch Church*. Spooky organ music is played by Jim Keyes as Jonathan Kruk begins his rendition of the tale that put Sleepy Hollow on the map. The place where the Pocantico crosses the Hudson River and flows into the Tappan Zee, in the words of Irving, *"continue[s] under the sway of some witching power. . .[that] holds a spell over the minds of the good people. . . the whole neighborhood abounds with old tales, haunted spots, and twilight superstitions."* Mesmerized listeners sit spellbound by Irving's words and Kruk's faithful evocation of Irving's iconic character—enjoying the experience in a church that had been old even when Irving lived here.

"America's first storyteller," Irving introduced the gothic tale to a fledgling nation in the early nineteenth century. The continent was, as yet, a much unexplored, unmapped, dark and mysterious wilderness in its abundant and mountainous woodlands (remember, the colonists had come from a largely deforested Europe), and Irving found in the landscape inspiration for his tales of mystery and terror. The colonists' fright of the unknown that hides among the tangling branches and creeping vines in the dark, deep forest, in the caves and precipices of the rough high hills is best conveyed by Irving in his account of *Rip Van Winkle*, an Everyman who is bewitched by mysterious mountain creatures when he wanders too far into the wilderness.

Westchester County still thrives on the legacy of Washington Irving. Until in 1996, when it decided to change its name to Sleepy Hollow, the town currently known as Sleepy Hollow was called North Tarrytown. Tarrytown is right off the Tappan Zee Bridge and is connected by Route 9 (Broadway) to Sleepy Hollow to the north and Irvington to the south. Route 9 is a hilly road where parking spots are at a premium; parallel to the road, and at the bottom of the slope, are the Hudson River and the train station. From the Tarrytown train station, the Metro North Railroad commuter train offers a convenient way to travel to New York City.

All of my Hudson River Valley destinations are within a few miles of the Tappan Zee Bridge, along Route 9. The route is lined with inviting small vintage shops and restaurants—Thai, Indian, and Italian among them, *Subway* being the only chain restaurant in sight. I particularly enjoyed the *Tarry Tavern*, where I savored the butternut squash soup and the squash and pear ravioli in a period setting.

My Hudson River Valley days typically begin with a New York bagel from the *Bagel Emporium* (which is across the street from my hotel), followed by a two-hour walk on the *Aqueduct* and over the estate of Lyndhurst. The *Croton Valley Aqueduct* that used to provide water to New York City is now a walking trail that follows the Hudson River from Sleepy Hollow to Tarrytown, passing through the *Lyndhurst* estate. It is a sliver of old forest in the town, with waterfalls and tall trees through whose thick fluttery veil of leaves sunlight comes through in fine streams; the cover of the leaves is generous enough that it kept me dry as I walked the trail during light early morning rain showers.

One afternoon I drove to the neighboring town of Irvington—to visit *Sunnyside,* the many-windowed cot situated on the bank of the Hudson, the house in which Washington Irving once lived. Having been devastated by the untimely death of his fiancé of consumption in 1809, then law-student Irving departed for Europe to attend to the family business. After a seventeen-year sojourn across the water, where he wrote most of the works we love so well, he returned to America a celebrity.

His Sunnyside home is a fairy-tale stone country cottage over which the tree branches reach, promising to completely cover it from view in time. Its sweetness calls to mind the alluring cottage of the witch in *Hansel and Gretel*. Irving's nieces, who lived with him in the old manse, loved séances, spiritualism, and crystal balls.

(For modesty's sake, nineteenth-century séance participants would touch a rope rather than join hands, the guide explained. He also said that people used to place a spoon under a table leg, which they could then press with their feet to cause the table to move up and down.) Poe, Scott, and Dickens were friends of Irving and visited him at *Sunnyside*. The docent threw out an interesting bit of gossip: after Dickens had stayed here and met Irving's relative Ebenezer, he wrote his own famous ghost story—*A Christmas Carol*—whose main character is named Ebenezer.

Snug Sunnyside's cozy rooms are small, gabled, and carpeted with soft furniture and warm textiles. The dining room table is set for a Van Tassel banquet with meats, fruit, and pastries. I looked for the doughnuts Ichabod loved so well. Irving's office holds first editions of the *Author's Edition* of his books. An exhibit displays many other incarnations of Irving's most famous story (including a cereal box).

I lingered after the house tour for the second and third performances I was to enjoy that week of *The Legend of Sleepy Hollow*. This annual evening affair at Sunnyside is called *The Sleepy Hollow Experience*. It includes a scavenger hunt and contest related to classic gothic fiction; among the clues are quotations from *Frankenstein*, *Dracula*, and *The Yellow Wallpaper*. Storyteller David Neilsen tells Irving's romance in an outdoor performance, and visitors can be photographed in Victorian mourning attire. As the sky grows dark, a handsome young Washington Irving takes his seat at a candlelit writing desk, penning his spectral tale while visitors gaze upon him with awe and take pictures of the author at work.

The sun is setting when the performance begins on the three-sided wrap-around porch of Sunnyside. Now illuminated by eerie red light, the quaint fairy tale cottage is decidedly scary. Ichabod, lantern held aloft, is wandering about as if looking for something, in a sort of agitated frenzy. He leads the audience around the corner to the Hudson River side of the cottage, where the changing red, blue, and green lights and spooky mist create a ghoulish atmosphere for the performance of *The Legend of Sleepy Hollow*, a musical re-telling of the beloved story. Photos are encouraged, and the audience is invited to participate. The performance takes place at four stages (the porch, the yard behind the house, the grove, and the horse path). At the Van Tassels' harvest party in the grove, the audience drinks toasts with the guests and characters pose for pictures with people in the audience. That evening one little boy was distraught—as he posed for a picture with Ichabod, Brom Bones knocked Ichabod's hat off his head. When the child burst into tears, Ichabod comforted him and told him that Brom was mean. The final act involves guests lining the horse path behind a fence, as the Headless Horseman gallops by, his terrifying pumpkin head tucked beneath his arm.

During my visit to the Hudson River Valley, I traveled twice by rail into New York City—to revel in two seasonably-spooky Broadway musicals (*Wicked* and *Beetlejuice*) and to taste other delectable Manhattan pleasures. A confluence of benevolent celestial influences had converged, it seems, to augment my adventures, for I was assigned a seat on the train beside fellow connoisseurs of the macabre—a garrulous brother and sister from Alabama who had come north to vacation in Salem and Sleepy Hollow. They were *Dark Shadows* aficionados, too, who had also visited the Lyndhurst mansion. We traveled convivially along the Hudson River in enthusiastic tête-à-tête about the rumored upcoming television resurrection of *Dark Shadows*. Fiendish luck continued to guide my course that day: the hostess at the *Metropolitan Museum of Art Dining Room*—whose five-star pumpkin-themed brunch is good enough to *die for*—seated me at a table next to that of another couple who love *Dark Shadows* and things horrific; they divulged to me that they had visited Edward Gorey's home in Massachusetts.

As my Hudson Valley Halloween was drawing to a close, I was positively oozing in creepy sentimentality—from having participated in this heartfelt communal fête of the classic American ghost story.

A Tale of Two *Dark Shadows* Mansions

The mysterious gothic Collinwood of *Dark Shadows* is not one—but three—mansions. Lyndhurst is the Collinwood of the two MGM films—*House of Dark Shadows* and *Night of Dark Shadows*. Seaview Terrace is the Collinwood of the original television series. Greystone Manor (in Beverly Hills) is the Collinwood of the 1991 *Dark Shadows* television revival series, which starred Ben Cross. I was able to view Greystone Manor from the street in the course of a Hollywood tour. It should be noted that the Collinwood of the 2012 Johnny Depp *Dark Shadows* parody was a stage set in England.

Lyndhurst

The neo-gothic architectural style—with its fanciful towers and arched stained-glass windows—evolved out of the very intense, emotional nineteenth-century Romantic rejection of the eighteenth-century emphasis on Reason. Lyndhurst is considered the premiere house built in the Romantic Gothic Revival style in America. Located in Tarrytown, New York, Lyndhurst was built in 1838 by General William Paulding, doubled in size in the 1860's by the second owner George Merritt, and eventually purchased by railroad baron Jay Gould. It has been featured in *The Men Who Built America*.

I had visited the mansion previously while attending *Dark Shadows* festivals in the summer. This time it was Halloween. On this frosty night, the venerable gothic mansion was creepily bedecked for the Halloween season. Viewed against the multicolored prism of the setting sun behind it, the green, red, and purple flood lights cast an eerie glow upon its gables, spires and turrets. A horde of zombies, created by students at a local school, were prowling along the twisting driveway that leads from Route 9 to the mansion. Spectral figures in translucent gauze haunted a grove of bare autumnal trees. Entrance to the grounds is free, and many people walk and hike the grounds and bike paths of the estate.

On the first evening of my excursion to the Hudson River Valley, I joined a throng of people in Halloween costumes—mostly families with children here to attend the performance of *Jay Gould's House of Curiosities* in the mansion; we were congregated in the Carriage House visitors' center. *The Addams Family* movie was playing and Halloween props were provided for photo-ops. A guide cracked Halloween jokes as he led the group up the candle-lit inclined path to the mansion. Once inside, he conducted us from room to room. Various *Addams Family* characters performed monologues. *Grandma's Kitchen* was the creepiest, as far as I was concerned, with a larder full of rats and spiders, and human body parts.

Lyndhurst was created with the aesthetic of vampires and unearthly spirits—simply perfect for the Collins family of Collinsport, Maine. A great gallery on the second floor features a high wood-beamed vaulted ceiling with buttresses, and a striped parquet floor. The dark, gothic carved woodwork provides a striking contrast to the white walls, and a dramatic background for the Romantic European paintings framed in sumptuous gold frames exhibited in this room: this was Jay Gould's own collection. At one end of the opulent gallery, five steps lead to the master bedroom. At the other end, a large floor-to-ceiling medieval arched picture window overlooks the Hudson. Suspended above a massive dark wood banqueting table in the center of the room is an imposing chandelier. Beneath this table little Sarah Castle hid when the adults arrived to seize Angelique for a witch. The green master bedroom is a weird polygonal shape, and it contains a bed engraved like an altar in a gothic cathedral—this was Dr. Julia Hoffman's room in *House of Dark Shadows. Here is the very desk at which she wrote in her journal a record of her blood experiments on the vampire Barnabas.* A canopy bed covered with intricately embroidered drapes and counterpane is in another bedroom; here the blue vaulted ceiling is sprinkled with gold stars and divided by gilt arches—it was inspired by *Sainte-Chapelle.* The State Bedroom is graced by a Tiffany window.

If you have seen *House of Dark Shadows* or *Night of Dark Shadows*, you will surely recall the weird octagonal, dark medieval dining room, with its curious table built to fit this unnatural space, into which young David Collins came running in to tell his family he has seen his cousin risen from the dead—a vampire—and that she had just tried to attack him in the pool house.

The high point of this visit to Lyndhurst was, for me—*The Tower.* I had not been able to view the tower on prior visits, for the tower is accessible only on the *Backstairs Tour. This time I had a ticket!* The Backstairs Tour is a curious walk through the kitchen (still cluttered with Grandma's accoutrements) and the separate laundry building (which contains the latest high-tech appliances of the 1890's and a dormitory for single servants). According to the guide, the Gould's treated servants rather like family, and staff accompanied the family on their frequent travels. The servants were largely recent immigrants—Irish, English, Russian, German, and French. In the 1860's, seven servants took care of the house, and fifty to one-hundred gardeners tended the grounds, many staying in a separate dormitory by the *Greenhouse.* Day workers lived in town.

The Tower Room was added by George Merritt as an astronomical observatory that overlooks the estate. It is reached through the three-story servants' wing, where on the third floor the senior staff shared with the family the modern full bath. Also on the third floor is a large guest bedroom and a smaller adjoining room suitable for a visiting large family with children and a nanny. The guide went on to tell us that the steep, rocky, swampy terrain on which Lyndhurst had been first erected was transformed by

Merritt and his master gardener into a horticultural masterpiece by the drainage of the swamp, the filling in of the crevices, and the planting of trees.

All of this was well and good, but by this time my heart was racing, for I was dying to enter the tower room—the unholy trysting place where the ghost of Angelique cast her spell to draw Quentin back into the witchy past, in *Night of Dark Shadows*. I yearned to see the closet wherein Quentin stowed his paintings—and the very place where he made love to his spectral paramour on the chaise. I was not the only one. Other tour participants were asking, "Wasn't *Dark Shadows* filmed here?" The docent confided that Lyndhurst was currently under consideration as a possible location for filming the revival of the *Dark Shadows* series on the CW network (in the works for 2020). As we entered the Tower, the sunlight rushed in with all its autumnal brilliance through the many floor-to-ceiling gothic windows on all sides. I lingered for a photograph before the closet of Quentin's illicit painting (despite the guide calling for everyone to come down the stairs). The ceiling in the Tower was abuzz—a genuine plague of flies darkened the ceiling, occasionally making a dive at one of us. Had this been a movie, I would certainly have recognized a cinematic and literary convention that foreshadowed evil —but this day the flies were real in the haunted tower of Collinwood.

After the conclusion of the *Backstairs Tour*, and the *Autumn Open House*, I walked the grounds of Lyndhurst, to the turn-of-the-century Pool House of marble and classical columns, now in a succulently, disturbing ruinous state (which featured in both of the MGM movies), and to the immense and now glass-less greenhouse, past the bowling alley building, the brick kennels, and the Rose Garden that contains over a hundred varieties of roses (some over one hundred years old). Stone statuary and seating areas provide locations for enjoying a view of the Hudson River.

As the sun rose on the final morning of my holiday in the Hudson River Valley I strolled to Lyndhurst. I bade Collinwood a daybreak farewell. I was about to embark upon a journey that would change my tomorrows. I was poised to drive to Newport, Rhode Island to visit *Seaview Terrace*—the mansion that was used for Collinwood in the television series *Dark Shadows*.

Seaview Terrace

I would be staying at Seaview Terrace. Here the exterior scenes of television's *Dark Shadows* were filmed. The interior scenes of the show were shot in an ABC studio in New York City, on sets designed to resemble the rooms of Seaview Terrace.

In the 1920s whiskey tycoon Edson Bradley purchased an Elizabethan manor-style house, *Sea View*, on Ochre Point in Newport; he then commissioned architect Howard Greeley to turn it into the stupendous forty-thousand-square foot gothic mansion known as *Seaview Terrace*. Today, Seaview Terrace—neighbor to the Bellevue Avenue mansions of the Vanderbilts, *The Breakers* and *Marble House*—is tenderly preserved by the Carey family. It is not open to the public. This was the tenth annual congregation of a throng of *Dark Shadows* friends, all of whom are indebted to the Carey's for allowing us to come home for Halloween.

It is incredible experience to drive up to the porte cochere, to pass through the grand, double timber doors, to enter the menacing gothic house atop the stony, storm-rocked Atlantic coast. Here Miss Winters came as governess to a child who was troubled—troubled by *spirits*, that is! I was assigned an attic room against which nor'easters beat and the widows wail as the wind forces itself through the chinks, making the brittle shades on my window go *thump, thump*.

The house has two towers, mullioned windows, and a terrace with a stone railing along its length. The East Wing faces the Atlantic, along the edge of which the *Newport Cliff Walk* sidles. Multiple gables, balconies, and French doors adorn this enigmatic edifice.

Inside is a gothic chapel—whose wrought iron French doors

open onto the terrace, and whose mirrored doors on the other side of the room open into the richly paneled dining room, where the iconic portrait of Barnabas Collins hangs over the fireplace. A portrait of phoenix Laura Collins and son David—painted among the flames in which every hundred years a phoenix must renew herself—sits in the recess of another stone hearth.

In the West Wing is the Great Hall where the ceiling is two stories high. Two gothic-style wooden balconies overlook this vast space. Resting upon the magnificent mosaic floor of the Great Hall is an enormous banqueting table. Suspended overhead is a chandelier that could have been purloined from a vampire's bastion. Portions of sixteenth-century sculpture pared from ancient European structures and exported to the United States—in the era when Gilded Age millionaires were making the *Grand Tour*—grace the walls and arched doorways. A long marble-and-blue hall—rendered tunnel-like by its series of Roman arches and made beautiful by its lacey latticework—spans the distance between the chapel and the Great Hall. Through the latticework one sees the winding gothic stone staircase to the second floor—and the high stained glass window beside it. Large, stone sixteenth-century fireplaces with carved faces that peer out at the unsuspecting visitor are found in numerous chambers. The house is so spacious that eighty seems like only a few people in residence. *I eagerly felt the paneled walls for sliding panels opening to secret passages.*

Many of the eighty guests are walking *Dark Shadows* encyclopedias. From all walks of life, they have in common a penchant for the macabre and a passion for *Dark Shadows*. At Seaview Terrace each night, *Dark Shadows* devotees convene to view the episode of *Dark Shadows* that had aired fifty years before on that date. One blustery evening, enclosed by the scrumptiously-molded white paneling and mirrored walls of the ballroom, guests were treated to a presentation of *Susperia*, a horror movie featuring Joan Bennett—a star of *Dark Shadows*—as the headmistress of a witch-infested ballet conservatory. *Dark Shadows* plays continuously on a television in the room known as the *Sixties Room* for its décor of lava lamps and day-glow posters. This intimate cell is also known as the *Angel Room* for its intricately-carved ceiling. And it is known to be haunted; it was featured in an episode of *Ghost Hunters*.

Damian the Magician performs magic shows and séances for his adoring Collinwood fans. *The Raven* is delivered by Frank, garbed in Edgar Allan Poe dark couture. In the solarium—where two great walls of floor-to-ceiling windows overlook the ocean, and French doors open onto the terrace—we each divulged how we had tracked down the mansion by our own sleuthing, surreptitiously viewed the estate from between the hedges, and eventually obtained an introduction to host Bob, who extended an invitation to enter our ancestral home.

On a previous visit I had dressed as the black-robed Leviathan Haza and carried a *Naga* box. This time I *became* Josette du Pres, bride of vampire Barnabas Collins. I wore Josette's wedding gown (recreated for me by a costume designer at my local community theater) and her signature jasmine scent. I carried the tinkling music box given her by Barnabas. Sometimes fans come as *Dark Shadows* characters Barnabas, Angelique, Dr. Lang, Elizabeth Collins Stoddard, Carolyn Stoddard, or Dr. Hoffman. A gallant guest swept me off my feet and waltzed me around the dance floor, whistling the iconic *Dark Shadows* tune *I Wanna Dance with You* from the 1897 storyline. At two o'clock in the morning, unwilling to let the lovely evening come to a close, my friend and I hula-hoop-ed on the moon-lit terrace in our costume-party gowns. The weather was unusually mild for the end of October.

Each morning in Newport *Dark Shadows* fans stroll the Cliff Walk along the Atlantic. As we follow the coastal path, we seek the place where the opening scene of *Dark Shadows* was filmed, the place where the camera had captured the foaming waves crashing upon the rocks. As we walk the path along the backyards of the Newport mansions we look for *Widows' Hill*, where forlorn women once waited for their sailor husbands who never returned home

118

to Collinsport—and whose wailing can still be heard, auguring inauspicious events. Some fans re-enact Roger Collins's loss of Burke Devlin's silver pen on the beach, which led to the discovery of his treachery.

Dark Shadows fans in Newport head to the *Black Pearl*, a seafood restaurant on the wharf which was used as the façade of the *Blue Whale* in the original TV show. Meandering around back of the building to the slips where the boats are docked, devotees imagine Barnabas biting pretty women's necks—or Hyde-like character John Yaeger running his blackmailer through with the sword concealed within his cane. Between events, fans swing on the seats attached to the gnarled old tree outside the terrace, or they visit haunted *Fort Adams*.

One fine morning I visited the *Redwood Library* and *Athenaeum* on Bellevue Avenue. Built in 1747 of wood painted to look like stone, it is the oldest continually operating library in America. A subscription library, it houses a fine collection of Gilbert Stuart portraits and eighteenth-century art—and, according to some sources, a goodly collection of ghosts, too. Some of the paintings are said to follow visitors with their eyes.

Next door to the Roman Doric temple façade of the *Redwood* is the fanciful frame structure of the *Newport Art Museum*. It has a wrap-around porch, a tower, polygonal rooms, Elizabethan beams, and a diamond-patterned roof. Constructed as the summer home of the Griswold family in 1864, it was purchased in the 1890's by the *Newport Art Association*, an association of women artist friends. Circa 1920 it became a general art museum exhibiting works from the 1980's to the present. The exhibit when I was there featured Winslow Homer prints—engravings he made for periodicals.

I next gathered up my *Dark Shadows* friend Vivian to visit three of the Gilded Age mansions for which Newport is renowned: *The Breakers, Marble House*, and *The Elms*. All three are sumptuous. The first two are characterized by late Victorian chic—heavy molding and heftily carved woodwork, massive gilt wood thrones and chairs upholstered in red velvet, ponderous étagères holding substantial globes, and red marble tables on overwrought pedestals. The Elms is a bit brighter and more graceful. In all these mansions the private rooms upstairs—while still elegant—are cozier, with delicate French furniture, tables, and woodwork in pastel colors. In all of the houses the ceilings seem to be in competition to be the best work of art produced by a reclining artist. These are only a few of the many "summer cottages" of the Gilded Age millionaires, which are now museums.

I returned to the Cliff Walk on my last morning at Seaview and watched the wetsuit-ed swimmers daring the frigid and frothy Atlantic waters. And then I shared brunch at the haunted *White Horse Tavern* with Amanda. The Tavern is a seventeenth-century Newport building, a red, barn-like structure with low, wood-beamed ceilings, a creaky wood floor, narrow stairs, colonial furniture, and built-in cupboards. I can see how it is that colonial ghosts are reluctant to leave this venerable establishment.

Driving homeward in eastern Massachusetts I passed a sign that read "1724 feet. Highest Elevation on Route 90 east of South Dakota." I put a *Dark Shadows* drama CD into the player and enjoyed more *Dark Shadows* on the way home.

H.P. Lovecraft's Providence

Once while Halloweening at Seaview Terrace in Newport, Rhode Island, I went for a day's drive to Massachusetts to see the *New Bedford Whaling Museum*, a national park that presents the history of the whaling industry and the culture that it spawned in New England. Whaling wrought its own destruction by hunting the whales nearly to extinction, first in the Atlantic and then in the Pacific. New Bedford is still a working seaport, and its sloping streets run down to the ocean where boats are docked everywhere.

Another time I went from Newport to Providence, Rhode Island. Providence was founded by Roger Williams. Himself a refugee from the Salem witch trials, Williams was an ardent proponent of freedom of religion. Providence is an old town, tightly packed on the slopes of its steep hills. Eighteenth and nineteenth-century Federalist and Greek Revival houses bordered by white picket fences grace the sloped and narrow brick roads. I spied a plaque designating *H. P. Lovecraft Square* en route to the *Rhode Island Institute of Design Museum*.

It is a curious museum consisting, in part, of the *Pendleton House* which houses their collection of seventeenth-century decorative-arts and furniture made in Newport, Boston, New York, and Philadelphia. Roman and Egyptian sarcophagi are here. Eighteenth-century lace is displayed in drawers in the costume wing. I saw a late nineteenth-century lace bodice that reminded me of *Phantom of the Opera*. I also spied a macabre twentieth-century Haitian beaded Voodoo flag. There is also a litter made of black wood with brass hardware in which, by means of poles, a Japanese bride

121

was historically transferred from father to husband. This eclectic collection is very Victorian in concept: in the nineteenth-century people were picking up all kinds of exotic and bizarre souvenirs from their travels and making their homes into miniature museums.

In the course of my most recent visit to Seaview Terrace I led a group of H. P. Lovecraft fans (Seaview friends Marge from Pennsylvania, Joe from Texas, and Jason from Nevada) from Newport to Providence to visit sites referenced in Lovecraft's stories or relevant to the writer's life. The weather was grey, the fog thick, and the atmosphere drizzled off and on all day—it was perfect weather for visiting the homes of Charles Dexter Ward and company. We visited *The Shunned House*, a weird four-story yellow frame house built right up close to the street. A huge tree that is taller than the house stands before it, seemingly trying to hide it from view. The door is shuttered, and the windows are placed asymmetrically, as if the blueprint had been drawn or the carpentry executed by a drunken constructor. There is no welcoming ornament—no wreath or door knocker—only shuttered door and curtained windows. Now known as the *Stephen Harris House* on Benefit Street, to Lovecraft fans it is the *Babbit House* (*The Shunned House*). Across the street from it is the *Old Court Bed and Breakfast*, which some scholars consider a possible inspiration for the home of Dr. Elihu Whipple in the same story. Along Benefit Street is also found the *Old Statehouse*, where in May 1776 Rhode Island became the first colony to declare its independence from Great Britain. Here is a peculiar old winding staircase: the guide told us that women prisoners were brought down these stairs from the third floor to the courtroom, and male prisoners were brought up from the lower level to face justice.

We enjoyed a visit to the 1838 Greek Revival-style *Providence Athenaeum*, where Edgar Allan Poe made love to his flame Sarah Helen Whitman, and where Lovecraft hung out; the *Athenaeum* is mentioned in several of Lovecraft's works. A bust of Lovecraft is accorded a place of honor in the foyer. We continued up the steep, close brick walks and street to the *John Hay Library*, where a plaque in front contains a quotation from *Fungi from Yuggoth*:

> *I can never be tied to raw, new things,*
> *For I first saw the light in an old town,*
> *Where from my window huddled roofs sloped down*
> *To a quaint harbor rich with visionings.*
>
> *Streets with carved doorways where the sunset beams*
> *Flooded old fanlights and small window-panes,*
> *And Georgian steeples topped with gilded vanes –*
> *These were the sights that shaped my childhood dreams.*

The *John Hay Library* owns the largest collection of Lovecraft manuscripts. The librarian offered us a box of facsimile copies of Lovecraft's notes and drafts of his stories, including street maps of Providence and diagrams.

We found on our wandering way the *Horace B. Knowles Funeral Home*—a grey-and-white frame building at which Lovecraft's funeral was held—and two Charles Dexter Ward houses: the *Henry Sprague House* whose Benefit Street address was used by Lovecraft for the location of the Ward house in *The Case of Charles Dexter Ward*; and the *Halsey House*, the building which was used by Lovecraft to describe Ward's home in the famous tale. The *Halsey House* has been considered haunted since Lovecraft's time.

As we sought Lovecraft's final home, the close and confined nature of old Providence was pressing itself upon my consciousness. The houses are close together, obstructing the sun and horizon; buildings loom over people in the labyrinth of streets. Living there would be like residing in a narrow, windowless corridor with numerous closed doors. Old Providence is a picturesque and suffocating garden in which Lovecraft's imagination thrived.

Lovecraft's final home, the *Samuel B. Mumford House*, is green with symmetrically placed windows and a Federalist-style fan-topped red door. A black wrought iron fence encloses the small front yard. Lovecraft utilized it for the house of Robert Blake in *The Haunter of the Dark*. We returned to our car parked by the *John Brown House* on Power Street (the first mansion built in Providence).

As we expanded our circumference, we found the *Fleur-de-Lys House* on Thomas Street, the home of artist Wilcox in *The Call of the Cthulhu*. The *Fleur-de-Lys House* was built by Sydney Richmond Burleigh, a Providence artist, and is fronted with bas-reliefs (a bas-relief figures prominently in the *Cthulhu* mythos). The house is eccentric in its green framing of yellow octagons and two-sided second floor windows that form wedge-like protrusions from the house in the manner of the prows on ships. The house is only a couple of doors from the *Providence Art Club*, which is often mentioned in Lovecraft's letters.

We lunched in modern downtown Providence and then visited the *Lovecraft Arts and Sciences* emporium, where I purchased a Shirley Jackson book, a CD radio drama of *The Dunwich Horror*, and a *Miskitonic University* window decal. We wound up our foggy, drizzly pilgrimage at the *St. John's Churchyard* on North Main Street. Poe and Lovecraft had each exhibited a predilection for the aesthetic pleasures of this graveyard. Although the stones are only knee-high, Lovecraft wrote in a letter that he and his friend lost each other among them. The flat tombs are quite sinister, suggestive of sacrificial altars and occult rites. Lovecraft's own grave is in the *Swan Point Cemetery*.

My *Dark Shadows* and H. P. Lovecraft-esteeming associates provided good conversation as we drove to and from Newport. Listening en route to Providence to the sound track of *Dark Shadows*, and on the return trip enjoying the soundtrack of the *Bram Stoker's Dracula* movie, we exchanged tales of Mercy Brown of Exeter, RI, who in 1892 was exhumed from her grave and subjected to actions designed to destroy a vampire; and of the *Bell Witch* of Adams, Tennessee, and other macabre tales (there was a wealth of stories between us).

124

With a heightened sense of anticipation, I traversed the Keystone State to cross one more item off my list of *Places that I Have Got to See*. Ever since having read in a footnote somewhere that Bram Stoker's notes for *Dracula* are housed in a Philadelphia library, I had planned someday to pay homage to these revered relics of the Greatest of All Horror Stories. How remarkable that a twist of fate has brought the notes of the Irish/English creator of the undisputed Sovereign of the Undead to America—and has deposited them in a library. This was my personal quest to the Unholy of Holies of macabre literature. A little research in preparation for my pilgrimage revealed that Philadelphia is the keeper of even more dark riches than I had known before.

As the sun rose on my first day in Philadelphia, I set out for the Vine Street location of the Philadelphia Free Library, where a knowledgeable docent inaugurated a tour of the Rare Books Department with the library's collection of Pennsylvania Deutsch *Fraktur*, a type of early American illuminated manuscripts. *Fraktur* artists would paint documents for framing, illustrating their borders to commemorate special occasions, such as the birth of a child or a wedding. We moved on to the Medieval illuminated manuscripts, and the docent explained to us about the use of vellum, an animal skin paper which enables texts to last a long time. He shocked our group of book lovers by describing the nineteenth-century practice of cutting the miniature pictures out of the illuminated manuscripts, to sell them or to paste them into scrapbooks.

I enjoyed looking at various other manuscripts in the eclectic collection that ranged from delightful to amazing—including a Beatrix Potter collection of first-editions, a 4,000-year-old Sumerian clay tablet, and a seventeenth-century Torah scroll. A letter written by Charles Dickens to Count D'Orsay about prison conditions, as well as a first edition copy of my favorite Dickens story, *A Tale of Two Cities*, are among the items in Dickens Collection.

The tour became decidedly more macabre now. The next item we viewed was an Egyptian papyrus from *The Book of the Dead*—an ancient guide to the spirit world, complete with pictures of mysterious falcon-headed figures and other Egyptian deities. In the course of the tour I added to my vocabulary a spooky-sounding word which does not, in fact, denote anything necessarily spooky: *incunabula*, which means books printed in the first fifty years of the printing press, dating from the invention of Guttenberg's press circa 1450 until 1500.

We had now reached the first of my two ghastly objectives, for which I had traveled from the Great Lakes Region to the Delaware Valley: the Edgar Allan Poe Collection. *The Cask of Amontillado* is given a place of prominence here: it is within the pages of an 1846 copy of *Godey's Lady's Book* opened to the story. There is a letter dated September, 1944, written by Poe; in it he writes of his wife's illness, tuberculosis. The raven Grip—stuffed now, but once the pet of Charles Dickens—is here. Grip was the muse for Poe's poetic masterpiece, *The Raven*.

The tour concluded in the library of William Mc Intyre Elkins, which was moved in entirety (books, furniture, fixtures, and walls) to the third floor of the Vine Street location of the Philadelphia Free Library, when it was left to the Philadelphia Free Library in Mr. Elkins's will.

The Rosenbach Museum Library on Delancey Court was my next destination. Here many people must experience déjà vu: scenes from M. Night Shamalyan's *The Sixth Sense* were filmed on this street.

The Rosenbach is in an 1865 house, owned and furnished by antique dealers before it became the home of the Rosenbach of today. Guests are required to put bags into lockers, wash their hands, and show their driver's licenses before entering. They are escorted from floor to floor, and may not move around out of the sight of the guardian of the rare books. A tour of the house starts with portraits of the family by Gilbert Stuart, in a room that also contains a wash stand which once belonged to Joseph Bonaparte, brother to Napoleon, and a 1700 cellarate, an elegant mahogany cooler for the newly- dreamt up champagne. The dining room has a marble clock made by Marie Antoinette's clock-maker: it is a tall white marble column, on top of which is a marble urn containing the clock; a brass band rotates around the urn to mark the hours, while the hour hand remains stationary. In the hall is the *Davenant Charter*, by which Charles II reopened the theaters in England. It is written on vellum and contains the provision that plays "may be performed by women," marking the first time that women were permitted to act on stage. A carved wood document box of unbelievable richness sits on a table beneath the charter.

In another room, a bookcase houses a collection of rare Melville books. The first Bible printed in the Americas is here, too: the *Elliot* (or *Indian*) *Bible*, printed in the seventeenth century in the Massachusett language of the Algonquin Indians, English letters used for transliteration of the Native American language. The Bible was intended for use in the conversion of the peoples whom the Europeans found already living in America when they arrived on the continent. The first edition of *Frankenstein* (1818) and also the first edition of John Polidori's *The Vampyre* (1819) are presented on the tour. There is even a poster, preserved from 1826, which announces the sale of tickets for the stage adaptation of *Frankenstein*.

I had made an appointment to spend individual time in the Reading Room to examine Bram Stoker's notes for *Dracula*—the Unholy Grail of the Macabre, and the second of my two objectives in journeying to Philadelphia. Stoker's priceless notes are written on linen rag paper, which is much more durable than wood pulp.

They are kept in mylar sleeves. These are all the notes known to exist. The librarian provided me a copy of Elizabeth Miller's facsimile of the notes with Miller's annotations to aid me in deciphering Stoker's hurried scratches and scribbles; an index at the back of Miller's book enables the reader to reconcile Miller's page numbers with the Rosenbach's. (The librarian shared with me that a new edition of Elizabeth Miller's facsimile is in progress.)

The *Dracula* notes were sold at auction in 1913, after the world had lost Stoker. They had been owned at one point mid-twentieth century by Charles Scribner. Their provenance is not complete. They had been attached to leaves similar to album pages but not numbered until they arrived at the Rosenbach, where the library worked to put them in order.

Stoker's notes range from full-size typed pages in which Stoker summarizes his research on Transylvania and superstition—including legends of vampires and werewolves, and the *unnatural* rules that govern them—to numerous two-inch by four-inch pieces of paper with hastily inscribed words—papers which had been folded up, presumably to put in his pocket, after he had jotted down his ideas.

That Bram Stoker was every bit as efficient and detail-oriented as his protagonist Mina Murray Harker is obvious when turning the treasured pages, for among the approximately one hundred twenty pages of his notes are found research on meteorology (clouds and winds), as well as recipes for Eastern European food. One page marked 1885 has a diary of the ship wrecks at Whitby. The collection includes newspaper articles clipped by Stoker, including the story of Mercy Lewis, the Rhode Island vampire. Here are also notes on the various effects of head injuries, relative to the parts of the brain harmed, which Stoker gathered in preparation for his depiction of the traumatic death of Renfield. Notable is a series of desk calendar pages which serve as a log of the action in the novel; the date Lucy dies is clearly marked on Stoker's calendar (29 September "Lucy's head cut off"). Stoker wrote outlines of the plot (which he divides into four books) and then individual pages with more detailed notes for each of the four parts. He began with a list of *Dramatis Historiae* from which were born some of the most memorable literary characters the world has known; some characters, however, never made it past the list. Stoker crossed off items on some of his lists. He wrote some scenes, then scratched some out, and then rearranged some.

The Rosenbach librarian then reverently returned her sacred charge to its protective box, and she presented the famous Nurnberg pamphlet, printed in 1488, which demonized Vlad Dracul, the Impaler. I was allowed to turn the pages! This incunabulum contains the most famous, infinitely reproduced, picture of Vlad. In it, the writer sets forth his indictments against Dracula's crimes. This document is largely responsible for Dracula's notoriety.

I find it tremendously satisfying that the Rosenbach loves these books as much as I do—and as much as millions of people do. I am obliged that it has shared them with me—Jane Q. Public, with no personal claim to these documents. The Rosenbach considers that all who love books and manuscripts should have access to their collection.

My Rosenbach day ended with a "Sleuths and Spies" hands-on tour. I was allowed to place my own hand upon a first printing of Poe's *Murders in the Rue Morgue* (1841)—the first detective story in the English language. The narrator is not named; the sleuth is a private detective; the police inept—a literary formula that still dominates mystery writing, the docent reminded the group. I reverently caressed in my hands an 1845 first edition of Poe's *Tales*. As I turned the pages in one of twelve installments of Dickens's *The Mystery of Edwin Drood*, I saw that half the blue-covered paper volume consists of advertisements for hair-restoration products, India waterproof overcoats, and similar goods. I lifted up and beheld the illustrations in a first edition of Arthur Conan Doyle's Sherlock Holmes stories. Among the last things I touched and looked upon were the final hand-written pages of Doyle's Sherlock

Holmes story, *The Adventure of the Empty House*, ready to be given to the printers, only a few sentences scratched out and rewritten, in Doyle's own elegant, precise script—*Arthur Conan Doyle had held those same pages in his own hands.* The remaining documents to which the group were treated were a love letter to Alicia Ripley, most likely written by Nathan Hale, a Revolutionary War spy (or by his brother); and some secret-code intelligence and hand-drawn maps of enemy installations, smuggled by Rose O'Neill Greenhow to aid the Confederacy, which contributed to the Confederate victory in the Battle of Bull Run during the Civil War.

My macabre adventures in the City of Brotherly Love were begun that morning with the Philadelphia Free Library tour where the docent quoted the Roman poet Horace. In his later poetry Horace proclaimed his victory over death—he wrote that he had achieved immortality through his work. Exertions of people to participate in the past and to interact with our intellectual antecedents is proof that Homer knew whereof he spoke. Great writers are the real Un-Dead, who come to life whenever they are beckoned—even long after they are buried. The Word spoken or written is immortal—it exercises living impact in the world. Bram Stoker and Edgar Allan Poe are present whenever their books are read. If that is not immortality, I don't know what is

Spirits with Stories to Tell in Gettysburg

In the first three days of July, 1863 America suffered its greatest loss of life in a single battle in Gettysburg, in a region of rolling, rich-green farmlands, a vast expanse of peach and apple orchards. In this bountiful land in the shadow of the Blue Ridge Mountains there were 51,000 casualties. Union and Confederate soldiers fell, their bodies hastily buried and later dug up again and reburied somewhere else; it is no wonder their spirits cannot rest. Many people believe this land is filled with distressed souls seeking peace. Considering the carnage they witnessed, the idea is not inconceivable.

My road-tripping friend and I are drawn to make the day's drive to Gettysburg and Lancaster County, Pennsylvania from time to time. The area has a calming influence. Life slows down in the city which retains its Civil War-era atmosphere, and in the surrounding villages and farms of the Pennsylvania Dutch country. It is difficult to not relax, futile to hang onto the sense of bustle. Cell phones do not belong here. This country encourages strolling, meandering, and pondering. It is a thoughtful kind of place. Perhaps it still channels the effects of the trauma that has forever scarred the American psyche, the PTSD of Cain and Abel. Gettysburg encourages a person to take time out for psychic healing, to remember griefs and make peace.

Gettysburg is a town of nineteenth-century brick buildings with porches and frame buildings with awnings shading the shop windows. On the porches of the shops are rocking chairs, and on the brick-paved sidewalks are benches for sitting awhile. The tourist traps are low-key, as if glitz and crass commercialism are considered in poor taste and out of place where so many were lost when our country committed fratricide. Gettysburg is respectful—even the ghost-hunters honor the pain of the wandering dead. Intimate coffee shops, antique stores, art galleries, wineries' retail storefronts, and souvenir shops make their homes in the nineteenth-century buildings. Life-size wax figures of our Commanders-in-chief are exhibited in the Hall of Presidents, where there are also smaller-scale replicas of the First Ladies in their inaugural gowns. A shiny, aluminum vintage diner is a good place for a quick lunch or a slice of cherry pie and a cup of coffee on the way to the nearby Lincoln Train Station, the place at which Lincoln arrived when he came to deliver the Gettysburg Address—which is now proclaimed every day in Gettysburg.

The Battlefield is why people come here. Something happens to you when you stand there quietly. To prepare for visiting the Battlefield, begin with the Visitors Center, which has a bookstore that sells a fine selection of quality literature on the Civil War, its causes and its consequences. The 1894 Cyclorama there is a circular mural with three-dimensional elements, a sight and sound experience to help the visitor gain a small insight into the battle. The film shown in the Visitors Center examines the complexity of the issues which Americans felt they could not solve except through warring against their fellow countrymen; although less than thirty minutes in length, the film dramatizes the difficulty faced by our representatives in government, so many of their constituents cherishing ideals and interests at odds with each other. A self-guided museum in the Visitors Center contains weapons and cannon balls, and soldiers' uniforms and personal effects. Exhibits shed light on the disastrous effect of America's growth spurt during the Westward Expansion that exacerbated tensions between conflicting interests—interests which had until that time been held in tenuous check: the fragile peace could not be sustained in the debate over whether states newly admitted to the Union would be slave states or free. From the Visitors Center, shuttles carry people to the Battlefield or take them to the Eisenhower National Historic Site, the home of President Eisenhower and his family.

We walked from the Visitors Center, breathing in the aroma of regret. Cannons stand retired in vast green meadows carved up by stone walls and split-rail fences, red barns and white farmhouses in the distance. Monuments of generals on horseback stand out against the horizon of a flat field. Markers commemorate particular military actions with legendary names such as Little Round Top, Cemetery Ridge, and Devil's Den. The Soldiers' National Cemetery is the resting place of more than 3,500 dead Union soldiers, half of them unidentified. The Soldiers' National Monument marks the location where Lincoln delivered the Gettysburg Address on November 19, 1863. It is a powerful place, charged with duty, honor, bravery, love, hatred, and grief.

The houses in the area are riddled with Civil War bullet holes, and with ghosts: the Jennie Wade House, the Shriver House Museum, and the Farnsworth House. We toured the Jennie Wade House (home to the only civilian who died in battle, Jennie being hit by a stray bullet) and the Farnsworth House, where we saw some of the Civil War bullet holes and heard the story of the family who lived there during the Civil War. That evening we returned to the Farnsworth where, in the Victorian Viewing Parlor, we heard stories of the ghosts who frequently appear to overnight guests. Several ghost tour companies accentuate the paranormal activity in Gettysburg, where the dead have many stories to tell. (The difference between ghosts and other dead people may be that ghosts initiate contact with the living because they have important things to say.)

We drove out from Gettysburg the next day through miles and miles—as far as the eye could see—of emerald flat farming land, hills occasionally gently rising and falling, and over all of it a cloudless blue sky; occasionally we spotted split-rail fences and plowed fields that were brown newly-turned earth instead of green-carpeted with crops. We drove past Pennsylvania Dutch farms selling homemade root beer and shoo-fly pie by the roadside, and we sat in the grass at one of them to enjoy some bread and jam. We stopped for a bit in Bird-in-Hand, a town with a small commercial center at the crossroads along SR 340; the town was named for the sign on a tavern which is no longer there. The Old Village Store has an old-fashioned checkerboard and sells nostalgic treats. We drove next to the Pennsylvania Dutch town of Intercourse, where we bought *I♥Intercourse* t-shirts, good for starting conversations in places where people have never heard of the town christened when "intercourse" referred to conversation and to intersections. We ate in an Amish restaurant and shopped in boutiques. Then we rode the Strasburg Railroad on a steam engine pulling antique train coaches. The National Railroad Museum of Pennsylvania is there, with its steam, diesel and electric locomotives; the visitors' center there is a Victorian train depot. On the Strasburg Railroad I always have a sense of the vastness of the earth—the green rolling hills of farms stretch to almost infinity from that vista—when buildings are few and far between (and only one or two stories tall when you do see them) there is a better chance of appreciating the breadth of the land.

Following our most recent trip to Gettysburg and Lancaster County we took a longer route home to visit the Flight 93 Memorial in Shanksville, Pennsylvania. In the mountains of the Laurel Highlands is a green field reached by driving high enough to feel it in your eardrums, up a narrow winding Route 30. The memorial center had not been built yet; there was just a plaza with kiosks honoring the passengers, their last words memorialized next to their photographs. Very high pine trees ringed the field—which was bare except for a large brown boulder that marked the place Flight 93 went down. Only families of the passengers and crew were allowed to approach the site.

A man on the road beyond the memorial site passed out brochures purporting that "Flight 93 was shot down;" a placard next to him was lettered "First Amendment Area." Much controversy surrounds the terrorist attacks of September 11, 2001. I am content that America is a place where people can voice controversial opinions with honest, open hearts and engage in meaningful discussions, where we can try to arrive at Truth together in conversation instead of on a battlefield.

Whether there was a conspiracy or not does not matter, though, when considering the altruism and courage displayed by forty average American people. Facing their imminent deaths, these heroic neighbors of ours put others first. They telephoned their families and loved ones to say their good-byes, they supported each other, and then they organized and overpowered the hijackers and caused the plane to go down in an empty field, preventing additional loss of life by diverting the plane from the terrorists' target. "Let's Roll" has become a potent American mantra, the emblem of the heroes who thwarted a terrorist assault when America was under siege, whose last breaths were spent fighting so that others would live.

This was a sobering journey, a necessary retreat. Gettysburg and Shanksville are hallowed ground, conducive to transcendent experiences, to glimpsing the universal, recognizing that there is something larger and that we are a part of it. Grief, admiration, sorrow, pride—these are emotions we comprehend. We sense in these places where terrible events unfolded something more profound, something even sacred. We come home from them more contemplative.

If ghosts are restless souls who have stories to tell, these are places where they would likely be found, for the spiritual energy is strong here. Paranormal experts attuned to psychic energy recognize that these quaint little towns and green fertile farmlands of Pennsylvania are electric with emotion. It is inconceivable that American idealism should perish.

Evans City Cemetery

"They're coming to get you, Barbara." We listened to the refrain of *Night of the Living Dead*, playing the DVD on the drive to Evans City, Pennsylvania just to hear the soundtrack. *Night of the Living Dead* is one of those movies for which I could finish most of the lines spoken by the characters. I drove with my friend. He owns a radio just like the one in the movie, over which the people barricaded in the farmhouse heard the breaking news reports of zombie movements and government-issued directives. It is really cool that all the towns mentioned in the movie's news broadcasts are near where we live.

Romero's masterpiece redefined zombie cinema: the screenplay, which he co-authored with John Russo, is not only about people versus zombies, as had been customary, but people versus zombies *and other people*. Despite the fact that little background is provided for the characters, their personalities are clearly expressed by their words and actions. As the zombies close in, the people in the farmhouse exhibit terror, cowardice, bravery, grief, and heroism—a microcosm of the human experience. The resourceful hero Ben comes up with several sound plans, one after the other failing for reasons beyond his control. Each time the viewer's hopes are raised they are dashed, and the zombie onslaught intensifies. People not only fail to cooperate, not only fail to come to each other's aid, but even set each other up for annihilation.

To reach Evans City, we drove along Route PA-19, about two hours through sparsely populated farmland where small clusters of two or three buildings occasionally break up the flat fields landscape:

every twenty or thirty minutes we would come to a restaurant or an antique store. Antique railroad passenger cars lounge in the grass at the Harlansburg, Station Museum of Transportation in Harlansburg, Pennsylvania on Route 19. A few more miles down the road, we came to a vast tractor graveyard that was featured in the movie *Staunton Hill;* here we rummaged through the mounds of tractor parts that reminded me of catacombs—tractor bones here are heaped up into piles like the caches of femurs and skulls in cathedrals.

At last we reached the Evans City Cemetery, where the opening scene of *Night of the Living Dead* was filmed. We stopped the car before entering the drive into the cemetery, pausing before the ground which is sacred to *Night of the Living Dead* fans. That driveway is the road Barbara's car rolls down as the zombie attacks her in her car (she does not have the keys to start the engine—they are in her dead brother's pocket).

We drove into the cemetery. It was a cold, blustery October day near Halloween. We sought the grave which belongs to Johnnie and Barbara's father, where they came to lay flowers on that fateful day. All of the cemetery is zombie-like. Headstones are helter-skelter in some places, and earth mounded up as if zombies are emerging from their graves and knocking the headstones over.

We walked around the chapel, so familiar to *Night of the Living Dead* fans, which in 2011 was supposed to be torn down because it had fallen into disrepair. Gary Streiner, brother of Russ Streiner who played Johnnie, enlisted *Night of the Living Dead* fans to raise the money needed to restore the chapel and save it from destruction. And then we played the parts of Johnnie and Barbara. We recited the mantras: "They're coming to get you, Barbara," "You have to shoot them in the head," and "Yeah, they're dead. They're all messed up," walking around the headstones, our arms stretched out before us, playing zombies, a couple of big children.

When we left, instead of putting the car in drive, we let it roll down the hill like Barbara did when she was fleeing the zombie who had killed her brother Johnnie. On the way home we stopped at a lonely cemetery, the only thing we could see in a sea of grass cloven by PA-19, and we walked around there for a while. We pretended that a lot of the people buried there had died in the same year, and we started making up stories about what had happened to them as the car took us home.

Shoot Them in the Head
Monroeville, Pennsylvania

Setting: the Monroeville Mall, a sprawling concrete box, just off the turnpike in the bosom of concrete Pittsburgh suburbia, June 2019. Shoppers in shorts, tank tops, and sandals, carrying plastic bags, wander the halls in small hordes.

Camera zooms in: the concourse outside Macy's lower level, where chairs are set up in rows around a raised dais, to the right of which is a bust of George Romero on a pedestal. To the left of the stage is a gothic castle photo prop, advertising a local haunted house attraction. People arrive and take seats, and also take photos of each other by the castle. One man is dressed like a vampire, with bat wings. Two little girls with white-painted faces and matching zombie outfits sit with their mother. Hordes begin to converge for the Living Dead Weekend at the Monroeville Mall, the place where *Dawn of the Dead* was filmed. This is the fifty-first anniversary of the greatest of all zombie flicks, *Night of the Living Dead*.

Above the stage, on the second level of the mall, are three rooms featuring stars of Romero movies (*Night of the Living Dead, Dawn of the Dead, Creepshow*), hawking photos, autographs, memorabilia, and action figures of themselves; the celebrities chat, sharing movie-making anecdotes with the fans. Interspersed among the actors are dozens of purveyors of ghoulish delights. Many sell books, which run the gamut from movie reference books to horror fiction. One author, John Borowski, writes about serial killers; he got his inspiration from Jeffrey Daumer. Other wares on display include t-shirts, costumes, masks, props, music boxes, jewelry, and posters. I buy two DVD's of old movies (*Village of the Damned* and *The Attack of the Fifty-Foot Woman*), my favorite type of creature-features. I am wearing my Quentin and Barnabas *Dark Shadows* t-shirt, which garners lots of comments from people who say they are *Dark Shadows* fans, too; the staffer who sells us our admission tickets shares that he is active in the *Dark Shadows* fandom, as well as *Night of the Living Dead*, and it turns out that we share some mutual *Dark Shadows* friends. We pass several booths promoting other horror movie events, such as the Creature Feature Weekend in Gettysburg. I have visited that solemn battlefield a number of times, but since having seen *Abraham Lincoln, Vampire Killer*, I have experienced a new, additional dimension of regret at all the needless carnage: had the armies recognized that they were fighting vampires and used silver ammunition, the war could have been ended much sooner.

John Russo has a prime location near the doorway; with George Romero, he co-wrote *Night of the Living Dead*. He is a gregarious man, happy to share stories about the zombie movie that started a landslide in American culture. Not only did he write the movie: he played two different zombies in it, changing his makeup after one was killed to play another. One of his characters is known as the "Tire Iron Ghoul." I ask him about the *Night of the Living Dead* script I own, autographed by Russo and dated "circa 1968," and John says that people like to buy the script because it has a different ending than the movie; they changed it during production. As he autographs a photo and a poster, he tells us that he had also written a screenplay for *Return of the Living Dead*, and when the producers decided to make it a comedy he was not very happy.

We say hello to lots of actors from the films, Adrienne Barbeau probably the most well-known, and end the day at the tables of the George Romero Foundation. I am very happy to meet Johnny (as in, "They're coming to get you, Barbara!") aka Russ Streiner. He autographs a still of himself and "Barbara" in their car in the Evans City cemetery, where the opening scene of *Night of the Living Dead* was filmed. Over the years, I have made several visits to that iconic landmark burying ground, in the small town of Evans City, Pennsylvania, where the Living Dead Museum can be found (and where they hold their annual October Living Dead Weekend). Russ signs the photo "They're coming to get you—Kathy!" and confides that they had borrowed his mother's car for the scene. A couple of people at his table ask him to speak to their friend on their phone, and he obliges a distant fan in that manner.

Gary Streiner, brother of Russ, is seated at one of the tables. He started the Living Dead Weekend. It was his efforts that saved the Evans City Cemetery chapel from destruction. My friend wants to know about the farmhouse used in the movie. Gary says it was torn down shortly after the movie was made, and that it had been a turf farm, and was now a cornfield. A dirt road off to the right of Ashtop Road, he said, will take you to the field the ghouls marched over into Evans City and cinematic history.

Ramona Streiner tells us that a 1973 Romero movie that has never been released before—*The Amusement Park*—is being restored, with the help of the Romero Foundation. Set in Westview Park, which no longer exists, but which used to be north of Pittsburgh, the movie was scheduled for release in October, 2019.

We bid farewell to the Living Dead world and exit the mall. Before we reach our car we pass an army surplus truck covered with blood, ragged zombies hanging all over the sides, and also a hearse with the license plate "DIGEMUP" and a window decal that says "Graveyard Mafia." Lots of fans are posing for pictures with the vehicles, savoring the moment. We have to leave, even though there are still two more event-filled days to the weekend, with tours of the mall highlighting places where scenes of *Dawn of the Dead* were filmed, including the mall rooftop, and a Monroeville Airport tour, complete with Helicopter Zombies.

Cried Witch in Holland, Michigan

It was a fine spring day, bright yellow sun in clear blue sky, as we drove the freeway past Battle Creek and Kalamazoo, en route to Holland, Michigan. There was no hint of danger—no dark and stormy weather; not a *Do not Trespass* sign, rather a road sign for a town famous for breakfast cereal; and a destination of tulips and wooden shoes. Little did I know that I would be cried witch before the day was out.

Holland is a town that was settled by Dutch immigrants in the mid-nineteenth century, and today is a tourist destination that offers a more convenient alternative for immersing oneself in Dutch culture than a costly trip to the Netherlands. We began that fateful day by visiting the Settlers House, which was actually built in 1867 by an Irish immigrant to Canada, but which represents the lifestyle of Dutch immigrants to Michigan in the second half of the nineteenth century; it is filled with furnishings from the time period. Then we went to Cappon House, which was built in 1874 and was home to Holland's first mayor, and is a fine Victorian house.

The De Klompen Wood Shoe and Delftware Factory was the next stop, a real delight. There I bought a pair of wooden shoes on which the date of our trip was added with a woodburning pen and a Delft pottery box with a picture of the Holland windmill. Visitors can watch the shoes being carved from blocks of wood on machines brought from Holland, and they can see the pottery-making process, from shaping the clay, to baking it in the kiln, and then painting the beautiful blue and white designs.

The Tulip Farm is an Elysian Field of tulips and daffodils. In

May, Holland holds an annual Tulip Town Festival, featuring flower shows and klompen-dancing people in traditional Dutch costumes. Women wear ankle-length dresses with shorter lace aprons and white lace collars and caps with pointed crowns and side flaps. Men wear short coats with double rows of buttons, wide-leg pants, caps, and neckerchiefs. Children in traditional costume ride on wagons in the parade.

De Zwaan is an eighteenth-century windmill in full operation in Holland, Michigan. Given to that city by the Netherlands, it is the only fully operational Dutch windmill in the United States, producing a fine-graham flour. We toured the inside of the multi-story structure and observed its mechanical operations. The blades turned by the wind cause the pole to rotate, and by means of belts and pulleys, wheels and cogs, large stone wheels turn to grind the grain. The guide pointed out bullet holes from World War II, when my friend's ancestors may have been shooting at mine, and I was thankful that that time was long gone, and there was no enmity between us now.

Our deceptively idyllic day continued with no signs of peril, as we headed toward the Dutch Village. Along the way we listened to a concert on *De Gouden Engel* (the Golden Angel) Street Organ; built in 1880, it is a pipe organ in ornate housing. The keyboard is in a box centered between two boxes housing the pipes, standing pastel porcelain figurines in front of the brass pipes. The wooden boxes are painted in pastels with gold framing. Originally, it had been made for a dance hall in Belgium.

The Dutch Village offers demonstrations in cheese-making and Dutch dance lessons. We stopped in artisans' shops and visited the Old Dutch one-room Schoolhouse. Unbeknownst to us, Fate was closing in. We came to the Weighhouse (*Waggebouw*), which did not look sinister in the least. In the seventeenth century, weighhouses were used to measure goods, because people didn't own their own scales. A building with a brick floor and whitewashed walls, it looked innocent enough. A large balance scale stood in the center of the room. If only I had remembered my history in time.

In the seventeenth century the Netherlands belonged to Spain, and the Netherlands were very hot. Hot as in burning witches. This period of witch hunts and the Inquisition in Europe is known as The Burning Times. Sixty-four people were burned over the course of a couple of months in 1613, as a result of the Roermond Witch Trial, in the Netherlands. For a long time before that, people had been accusing each other of being witches when babies died, or cattle, or people were afflicted with rashes, or crops failed. People were accusing their neighbors of practicing malicious magic. Beneficial magic had been traditionally accepted (people, for instance, had, for as long as could be remembered, sought out magic healers for cures for their illnesses) until the Catholic Church began to crack down upon all magic. Fueled by the Inquisition, all evidence of magical activity was linked to pacts with Satan. Torture, along with various other tests of guilt or innocence, preceded death by drowning or burning. Tests included throwing accused witches into water, where if they floated they were found guilty and if they sank they were posthumously declared innocent. The accused were said to have sex with the devil at their Sabbaths, at which cats and dogs, and goats and hares, would take part.

The woman who operated the scales told me that I looked like a witch, that I looked as if I were lighter than I really was. She explained that if a person weighed less than she appeared, then her bones were hollow and she could fly, proof of witchcraft. I stepped upon the scale, a wooden platform held by four very thick ropes which converged together at the tops, where the fulcrum was; on the other platform, the wicked woman piled lead weights until the scale was balanced. Anxiously, I awaited her verdict. She said I was innocent of the charge of witchcraft, for I weighed no less than I looked. And she gave me a "Certificate of Proof of Innocence of Witchcraft" which stated that my "Weight being commonly found at that place, and in accordance with the natural proportions of the

Body," I was innocent. I was encouraged to produce the certificate as needed, whenever I found it necessary to prove that I was not a witch. It was signed by the Burgemeester.

StokerCon 2019

StokerCon 2019 took place at the historic and haunted Amway Grand Plaza Hotel, in Grand Rapids, Michigan. I attended this convention of the Horror Writers Association with a friend I met through the *Dark Shadows* fandom, Amanda Trujillo, who has a first novel in publication. Registration included a t-shirt, with the convention logo of a gothic tower rising out of the Amway Grand Plaza building, and a souvenir anthology book of articles, stories, and poems by HWA members. Attendees included both horror writers and horror fans.

The first session I attended was a panel called "Good and Evil and Life and Death," in conjunction with the Ann Radcliffe Academic Conference, which was embedded within the larger umbrella of StokerCon. In this session, Amanda presented a survey of psychic detectives in fiction and television; she described their evolution in response to various social changes over time, from the nineteenth to the present century. The other papers in the session were fresh takes on *The Exorcist*, Gavin Hurley focusing on the novel's dialectic aestheticism and Michael Potts on Chris's profound fear of death, a symptom of her atheism; both authors agreed the style of the novel forces the reader to actively engage in a contemplation of the nature of good and evil. My next stop on this delightful tour of the world of horror was Tim Waggoner's writing workshop, "The Art of Suspense," part of the Horror University portion of StokerCon.

Day two began with the Librarians' Day part of StokerCon, at the opening session of which I met Dacre Stoker, the congenial great-grand-nephew of Bram Stoker, who autographed my copies of his books (the sequel and prequel of *Dracula*) and posed for photos; and we had a nice conversation about his other projects (a movie deal with Paramount) and his guided tours of Transylvania and Ireland (Bram's birthplace). I had come here primarily to meet the blood-descendant of Bram Stoker, the carrier of the torch, the bearer of the Dracula legacy. Dacre explained that Bram was one of seven children, and that he himself was descended from Bram's brother George. Dacre, and J.D. Barker (co-author of *Dracul*) presented "Even Immortals Have Their Beginnings: the Research and Writing of *Dracul*."

Dacre told the audience that while he was researching *Dracul* (the new prequel), he came across Bram Stoker's lost journal in the attic of a house on the Isle of Wight: written when Bram was a college student, the journal entries presage the creation of *Dracula*. Dacre and Barker agree that Bram Stoker believed in vampires and believed that Dracula was real, and that Bram Stoker wrote *Dracula* as a true story, a warning, in fact. Dacre stated that Bram's English publisher excised the first one hundred one pages of the novel before publication, to strip the realism from the book; these excised pages are the focus of *Dracul*, Dacre's prequel to *Dracula*, in which Bram Stoker is the protagonist. (The only known typescript of the novel is missing the same 101 pages, and one can see where the pages have been physically cut out, or have been crossed out; found in a barn in Pennsylvania, the manuscript had been brought by Bram to the recipient as a gift. The well-loved story *Dracula's Guest* is part of the missing pages.) According to the writers, Stoker sent the uncut, more complete version of *Dracula* for publication outside of England. The intact *Dracula* was published serially in Iceland, and Dacre has had this version translated into English, wherein the material of the missing 101 pages can be found. A new, more complete version found in Sweden and translated into English is forthcoming. Dacre reminded the audience that Bram had himself cremated, most likely to avoid vampirism: "There are mysteries men can only guess at," Bram wrote.

Stoker and Barker also described some of Bram's life experiences that found their way into *Dracula*. They told how Bram's imagination (as a bed-bound boy who was subjected to bloodletting as a standard medical treatment) was formed by stories told by his mother and nanny about the cholera epidemic and Irish vampires (*Dearg-Due*). In the course of the cholera epidemic, 15,000 people fled Ireland and 1,500 died, and there were numerous instances of people thrown onto piles of corpses, when they had not yet died, and who were subsequently observed to rise from the dead. Fearful people would sit in front of their houses wielding long sticks, to prevent other people from getting close. Dacre then explained that *Dracula's* characters are based on Bram's family members and acquaintances (i.e. sister Matilda is Mina); and the spine of the hardcover edition of *Dracul* reproduces a drawing by Matilda, who was a successful artist. Seating charts from Beefsteak Club dinners indicate that Bram's social circle included Hungarian Ambassador Grushen, and Arminius Vamberry (a source of information on the mythology of eastern Europe), as well as Henry Irving and other Lyceum Theater associates. This absorbing lecture—and the opportunity to meet the blood descendant of Bram Stoker—was well-worth a three hundred-mile drive.

The next event was the "Historical Horror: Inspiration, Research, and Storytelling" panel about writing horror stories about real historical events. Panelists emphasized historical accuracy, as readers love to bring it to a writer's attention when he has not got his facts straight. They also discussed methods for maximizing the research time necessary for historical writing, as well as whether certain topics (i.e. rape) or events should be avoided, and how to use sensitive issues without exploiting them.

After that, I attended the "Ambiguously Haunted Houses" panel. Author Kathe Koja spoke of the ambiguity of *The Haunting of Hill House*, a novel seen through the eyes of Eleanor, whom she characterized as malignant, and not a victim. Koja said the long sentences of the novel help to hold the reader in its world. The panelists discussed the 1963 and 1990 movies, and the 2018 Netflix movie. Everyone agreed that they liked the earliest the best, disliked the 1990 version, and agreed that the 2018 version dropped the investigative aspect completely, in favor of straight horror. That the house is the main character of the novel was the consensus. Also on the agenda was *The Turn of the Screw*. My friend Amanda held that the governess is not mentally ill and notes that the house is a character, too—it reacts to the other characters, and the characters react to the house. She pointed out that Henry James's brother was president of the Parapsychological Research Association. In the 1974 movie, Amanda said, Dan Curtis's governess is not attracted to her employer (as are the governesses in the other movies), and she even tells him that he is a horrid man. The panel agreed that these tales of ghost-infested houses are enduring because the reader can never get to the bottom of the questions of whether the houses are victims or perpetrators of malignance, and that their ambiguities allow the reader to project their own anxieties into the stories.

Another stimulating discussion took place in the "Creature Features" session. The authors on the panel explained that monsters force us to remember that we are not always predators, that in our genetic memory we know we have been prey. Fighting monsters also affords us the opportunity to win against bad guys, if we are tough enough or smart enough. Another way of winning against them is to "defang" them to turn them into parodies (like *Sesame Street*'s *The Count*), enabling us to rid ourselves of our fears. This process requires continually inventing new monsters, or using the same monsters in new ways, in order to continue being able to terrify readers. I also attended sessions on "Research and Writing Horror Nonfiction," and sessions on writing short stories and novellas, and on audio books. These sessions covered technical, as well as market, topics and offered tips for getting published.

"120 Years of *Dracula*," a second presentation by Dacre Stoker, commenced with a brief biography of Bram Stoker, incorporating exciting new information yielded by Dacre's investigation into the roots of *Dracula*. Dacre's sleuthing has yielded such fruit as identification of the very books that Bram used in the London library—the margins of these books were marked by Bram Stoker with Xs and double Xs in places and show where he found information on vampires and Transylvania. When Florence Stoker's lawyer, Dacre said, told her that *Nosferatu* was being shown again in Berlin (despite the court's order that all the copies of the movie be destroyed, because the story had been plagiarized), it was already too late, as Florence had sold the *Dracula* movie rights to Universal; Hammer Studios later bought the rights from Universal. Dacre took us on a swift jaunt through pop culture obsession with all things *Dracula*—from movies to comics, car commercials, and cereal boxes. Dacre took a moment to say that the television show *Dark Shadows* was a particular favorite of his; he even acknowledged the fans, some of whom were in his audience, who helped preserve the Newport, Rhode Island gilded age mansion Seaview, which was used as the Collinwood of *Dark Shadows* on television.

Although there were many panels, presentations, and workshops I could not attend—for I had no doppelganger to deploy—I benefited from several more workshops and panels, and met and obtained autographed books and photos from a number of authors. Eleventh-hour entertainments concluded each day's programming; these ended at the stroke of midnight. One night closed with Josh Malerman staging a reading of *Unbury Carol* and other works, with acoustic guitar accompaniment, and actors presenting surreal manifestations of the text as he was reading. The subsequent evening Kathe Koja conducted an audience-participation creation of *The Art of Darkness*, in which I felt like I was part of a poem, myself all mixed up in it, my personal boundaries blurring with the art.

The Final Frame Short Film Competition of the next-to-last evening was an emotional roller coaster ride through vales of horror, as we were treated to a marathon of *very* short high-impact horror

150

films. On the last night, as we were gathering outside the ballroom for the banquet and ceremony which accompanied the presentation of the annual Bram Stoker Awards, a bartender pouring my chardonnay told me that a little girl's ghost had been seen many times on the Patlind (older) side of the hotel, and that in 1986 the Amway serial killer had take several guests off-premises and killed them. During the banquet, I sat at a table with Amanda; John B. Kachuba, a member of the Ohio HWA chapter (who tells ghost stories at Ohio libraries in October, and who gave me his book *Ghosthunting Ohio*); North Carolina writer Michael Potts, who writes really creepy horror poetry and novels about demonic possession; and Welsh writer Howard David Ingham, who writes nonfiction about folk horror, and who is translating the eighteenth-century Latin document, the *Berith Pact*, an occult text making a pact with a demon. The opening remarks were made by the speaker Jonathan Maberry, who has risen to literary success, despite parents who discouraged him from reading. When a boy, a school librarian had taken him under her wing and introduced him to writers who would became his mentors: Ray Bradbury, Richard Matheson, and Arthur C. Clarke, among others. He continued the theme that the Horror Writers Association is a family, and encouraged our mutual support and mentorship. He told us not to fear our most horrible thoughts: "Those thoughts are worth money."

Prelude to Ape Apocalypse
Dayton, Ohio

In Ohio's heartland is Dayton, usually a quiet home town, a close-knit community in southwestern Ohio farm country, once home to Orville and Wilbur Wright, who pioneered aviation in nearby fields. Now the Air Force Museum is there, celebrating the beginnings of American aviation with the Wright brothers and the milestones of flight achieved since that time. Driving around Dayton the visitor comes to the original buildings of the Oregon Historical District, now the entertainment center of Dayton, where umbrella tables are invitingly set up on the sidewalks outside the restaurants and pubs. The Citizens Motor Company is a restored Packard dealership, where auto mechanics still can be found working on vintage cars. The Huffman Prairie Flying Field is the place the Wright brothers developed their planes, and the Wright Cycle Company is the brothers' original store. On this day I drove to Dayton with my friend to see the Air Force museum.

The Dayton National Museum of the United States Air Force and IMAX movie center showcases American strength and ingenuity—from the *Gemini* spacecraft and Apollo 15 command module *Endeavor* to stealth bombers. It features a hot air balloon and dirigible. There are De Havillands, Fokkers, and Sopwith Camels. Galleries display World War II, Korean War, Southeast Asia, and Cold War aircraft. The museum recognizes the heroism of American service women and men with an exhibit of proudly-worn uniforms and medals and dioramas of Air Force personnel at work defending our nation. Among the more than

400 aircraft on display are planes which carried Presidents F. D. Roosevelt, Truman, Eisenhower, Kennedy, Johnson, and Nixon. One of these planes carried the Kennedy's to Dallas and returned to Washington D.C. with the body of John Fitzgerald Kennedy and a new President.

As the visitor reads the stories attached to these flying machines the grim reality underlying the bravery of the fliers and the technological achievements of the engineers becomes clear. The Boeing B 29 *Superfortress* on display deployed the *Fat Man* atomic bomb on Nagasaki. The Boeing B-17 F *Memphis Belle* is a veteran of the desperate bombings which nearly destroyed Europe in World War II. The glory of victory in war always has the flip-side of suffering and destruction, the real-life horror that fiction is always trying to represent in its various monsters.

The missile silo houses ICBMs (intercontinental ballistic missiles). The pointed noses of Minuteman and Titan missiles strain at the sky, arranged in a circle in a Tower of Babel-esque silo. The human race has achieved an ungodly destructive capability. As I stared up at the tops of the missiles, I felt cowed as a peasant girl who dared look up at the gigantic Athena in the Greek Parthenon. I have not since that visit been able to recall the Air Force Museum without envisioning Charlton Heston in *Planet of the Apes*, crying, "You blew it up! Ah, damn you! God damn you all to hell." Oh, the dreadfulness of that missile silo, that temple to the god of war, the power to destroy life as we know it at the push of a button.

The Dayton National Museum of the United States Air Force, like Heston in *Planet of the Apes*, shrieks Cassandra-like to all who will heed a warning against self-annihilation, suicide by apocalypse. In that missile silo I came face-to-face with the demonic creature who lurks within ourselves, and Heston's agonized scream reverberates as an echo in a close chamber every time I picture those towering, shiny, white, and hard ICBMs.

Wicca is Alive and Well in Cleveland

P ark your broomsticks on Broadview Road in the artsy, ethnic, and eclectic Old Brooklyn neighborhood of Cleveland, Ohio, and visit the *Buckland Museum of Witchcraft and Magick*, where museum owner Steven Intermill will tell you about the cache of artifacts collected by the founder of American Wicca, Raymond Buckland. Born in England to a family of Romani heritage and occultist leanings, Raymond Buckland had studied Wicca there under Gerald Gardner (1884–1964), the father of modern Wicca. Buckland collected occult objects, which were first housed in a New York City museum in his own basement from 1966–1976, and then moved to New Hampshire, New Orleans, and eventually Ohio, where Buckland settled at the end of his life. Now they are housed in this Cleveland museum.

Buckland's own spiritual journey coincided with the revival of the *Old Religion* in England, which was highly publicized through the efforts of Gerald Gardner. With the 1951 repeal of the Witchcraft Act of 1735, the practice of witchcraft became legal in England, and Gardner proclaimed a resurgence of the ancient, nature-based Old Religion known as Witchcraft or Wicca, terms he used interchangeably to betoken the age-old concept of Wise Ones, who knew the secrets of healing and protection. Along with anthropologist Margaret Murray (author of *The Witch-Cult in Western Europe*, 1921), Garder explained that although the Old Religion dating from Paleolithic times had been forced into hiding by the establishment of Christianity as a state religion, it had never disappeared. He claimed that ancient

154

Wicca harkened back to the horned gods and fertility goddesses of the Stone Age peoples.

In 1962 at the age of twenty-eight, Buckland moved to the United States. Deciding to become a Wiccan, he went to Perth, Scotland to be initiated into the Craft by Monique Wilson, High Priestess in Gardner's coven. When Buckland returned to the United States, he brought Wicca with him. His wife Rosemary was initiated into Wicca, and together they started a coven in Long Island. In 1964 Buckland began to accumulate artifacts for a witchcraft museum. Museum owner Steven Intermill told us they had recently celebrated Buckland's feast day, the second anniversary of his passing to the Summerland.

Buckland distinguished between the terms *Wicca* and *Witchcraft*—the first he used to refer to the worship of gods and goddesses of the ancient nature-based Old Religion; the second he used to refer to the ceremonial magicians whose focus is on the casting of spells. Buckland was a prolific author, publishing over sixty works on Wicca and Witchcraft, and he frequently expounded upon his spiritual views in television and print periodical interviews. In 1986 he published *Buckland's Complete Book of Witchcraft*, a sort of "Witchcraft 101" textbook, which explains the underlying concepts of Wicca and the worship of the *Lord* and *Lady,* the male and female principles in the natural world. His "Big Blue Book," as it is usually called, has been in print ever since, and is considered a classic in the genre.

I purchased a copy of Buckland's "Big Blue Book" in the museum gift shop, where I perused the wares with the two friends who had accompanied me on this expedition whereby we inaugurated the macabre festivities of the merry month of October. In addition to a large selection of occult literature, both fiction and non-fiction, the shop features runes, crystals, tarot, poppets, wands, candles, and dream-catchers.

Buckland's purple ceremonial robe is displayed in a showcase visible from the entrance into the museum. In a case to the left of the robe is Buckland's ceremonial horned helmet, which he fashioned from a hardware store cooking pot and toy animal horns. (Intermill explained that objects are more powerful when crafted by yourself and infused with your own magick). The silver crescent moon headdress worn by High Priestess Rosemary (Lady Rowan) Buckland is there. A green spiral-bound notebook contains Buckland's hand-written draft of his *Complete Book of Witchcraft*.

Suspended from the ceiling is a well-used broom. I asked Intermill how many miles were on the broom, and he replied, "A lot—it's been around the world." I noticed a shadow-box containing a doll-size outfit consisting of a shawl, a blouse, and a red skirt with white polka dots. Intermill told us that his mother had said she had a special gift for him to display in his museum (causing him some concern as to the appropriateness of her contribution). He continued by saying that he had been pleasantly surprised when she presented him with this representation of the Swedish *Paskarringar* (Easter Witch) tradition, wherein little girls dress up in witch ensembles of scarves and oversized skirts and shawls to seek treats from their neighbors (as American children do at Halloween). The tradition had evolved from an old legend that annually on Holy Thursday witches would fly on their broomsticks to attend a witches' convention, and when the sorcerers returned to Sweden they would find the people had prepared bonfires to make them think twice about landing there. Bonfires are still lit on Maundy Thursday in Sweden.

A white magic circle is painted on the black floor, with mysterious occult symbols and other glyphs signifying the four cardinal directions. It was painted by a member of the Art Department at New York University. Intermill told use that one day he was standing in the circle and joking with friends about Beelzebub and flies, after which he was beset by a veritable plague of flies for a period. Subsequent to that experience, he allows no jesting in the circle and counsels caution within its circumference.

On the wall is a collection of *William Mortensen's Witches*, on loan from the New York City *Stephen Romano Gallery*. Mortensen developed the art of photo-shopping when he was working with film in silent-movie era Hollywood. He earned a scandalous reputation for himself through his pursuits of his two predilections—macabre art and his paramour Fay Wray. Beautiful witches, hags, and wizards—in various shades of black and white and stages of undress—fly over conical medieval towers on broomsticks or skulk amid eerie paraphernalia in gothic settings.

Brass Chinese Zodiac symbols hang on a wall near the necromantic wand of Aleister Crowley, a colorful occultist contemporary of Gerald Gardner who proclaimed himself messiah of the *Nu Aeon* and antichrist. A Beatles *Sergeant Pepper's Lonely Hearts Club Band* album cover is exhibited: among the faces pictured in the crowd are Aleister Crowley and Edgar Allan Poe.

The head of a long-horned, long-bearded black goat is mounted on the wall in an area featuring psychedelic *Age of Aquarius* articles from the late 1960s and early 1970s, when divination and Zodiac parlor games were popular among people of all ages. Ouija boards, tarot cards, and children's toys with magic eight-balls are displayed with Day-Glo fluorescent paintings and black lighting. I asked Intermill whether the sofa in that area had some significance (it is of the same time period), and he told me that it is for spouses who are not "into" the magick and who are waiting for their better halves to finish looking at the museum.

Black mirrors for scrying the future or contacting spirits are scattered throughout the museum, as well as *athenes* (ceremonial blades). A 200-year-old mandrake root is there, carven into a female fertility image. A brass box bound with a cord is in a case—it contains a demon trapped by Buckland, who came to the aid of a friend who had mistakenly called the demon forth and who could not send it back. A placard warns not to say the demon's name, lest it become active once more.

Taking leave of the museum and Mr. Intermill, we crossed the street to eat at *Lucy's Ethiopian Restaurant*. We sampled a sweet, but by no means cloying, Ethiopian honey wine and traditional dishes of potatoes and carrots and lentils, which were served on platter-size circles of spongy bread. Instead of using utensils to carry the savory morsels to our mouths, we were instructed to scoop up the food with the bread. After we finished our delicious meal, the server brought a wrought-iron pan of smoking coffee beans, roasting them right at the table, and a bowl of sweetened popcorn. The server returned to take the beans to the kitchen and prepare the coffee. Ethiopian coffee is rich and dark, but not bitter. At *Lucy*, it is served in a traditional round-bottomed clay vessel with a thin neck. The coffee is poured into demitasse cups. Incense is included on the rattan tray with the coffee, sugar, creamer and demitasse cups and spoons. Diners can replenish the incense in the burner as it burns off.

The Halloween season was off to a great start: we compadres had plans to convene again in a couple of weeks at *Lawnfield*, the Mentor, Ohio home of President James A. Garfield, for a tour of the house and for a performance by an Edgar Allan Poe interpreter presenting *Hop Frog* and *The Raven*. 'Tis the season.

Lurking in Savannah

I visited Savannah, Georgia to see its historic homes, enjoy some genteel Old South atmosphere, appreciate for myself just how deserving it is of its reputation for eccentricity, and experience the Bonaventure Cemetery. My hotel was on the Savannah River; in fact, an ocean-going vessel piled high with hundreds of box cars was docked right outside my window. It is a busy river, and there were numerous ships as large as the one parked by my window. And along the river is a river walk, old cotton warehouses now souvenir shops, confectionaries, restaurants, and taverns.

My hotel was on the higher ground above the river, and the view was spectacular. Although it was a cold and windy November day, colder than I had expected in the Deep South, I spent the day walking the streets, shopping for dresses in small and elegant boutiques, sampling the wine selection in a lounge with a Gatsby feeling—matte teal blue walls, chrome bar shelves and furnishings, Art Deco geometrical light fixtures, and bartenders wearing bowties and suspenders. The city is punctuated by twenty-two squares of large, open gardens with monuments and benches, small parks only blocks apart. I walked around the Colonial Park Cemetery; notorious for ghostly orbs and voodoo practices, it features prominently in ghost tours of Savannah and television documentaries. I photographed the sidewalk, clay tile squares impressed with piano-key borders surrounding center squares filled with four concentric circles. On a monument by the cemetery I saw a sign that stated that it had been erected by the Daughters of the American Revolution in 1913. I ate at a brick-walled restaurant, *Alligator Soul*, featuring fantastic paintings in vibrant colors. When I returned to my hotel, I took in the beautiful view of the Savannah River illuminated at night by the lights from the riverbank. Parallel lines, colored white and green, stretched languidly across the ripples of the black-green water, a dreamlike collaboration of nature and art.

The next day my walk had a more definite agenda—the historic homes. My first stop was the 1816 Owens-Thomas House, a yellow English Regency house in Savannah known for its acanthus scroll supports; the guide identified the slave quarters and discussed relations between the social classes, as well as the use of locally-available building materials. I walked down Savannah streets overhung with live oaks, the trees providing a dollop of marsh-like sensibility to city living, especially with the profusion of large-leaf green plants and bed after bed of luxuriant flowers in the yards of private homes and in the great squares.

I toured the red brick Mercer-Williams House, made famous by John Berendt's novel *Midnight in the Garden of Good and Evil.* Wrought iron balconies around white double full-length arched windows peek out from an abundance of palms and deciduous trees that seem to be holding the house in check, asserting the primacy of nature. A wrought iron fence surrounds the property, grey stone steps leading to a white front door flanked by double columns. A surfeit of flowers seems to anchor the house, to be holding it in place; nature flourishes in this garden town, struggling to reclaim it from the buildings. The house had been abandoned and was in a state of serious disrepair when John Williams bought it, and he lovingly restored it to grandeur. Williams's life's work was resurrecting dead houses, breathing life into architectural corpses. Mercer-Williams, like so many other houses, has an enclosed courtyard, thick with moist green vegetation: not even expert landscaping can mask the sensation that the marshland is asserting itself through cracks in the streets and the foundations of fertile Savannah.

The Sorrel-Weed House is a Regency Period Greek Revival yellow house with green and white shutters. It is known as the most haunted house in Savannah (per ghost tour companies and television ghost-hunting shows) for untimely deaths and ample paranormal activity. I finished the day with dinner at 1790, an elegant red-brick, low-beamed restaurant in an historical building with a stone floor and crystal chandeliers—and according to the staff, plenty of ghosts.

The Telfair Museum was my first destination the next day, for it is the home of the *Bird Girl* sculpture by Sylvia Shaw Judson. The *Bird Girl* became celebrated after appearing on the cover of *Midnight in the Garden of Good and Evil.* When the book was written the sculpture had been located in the Bonaventure Cemetery; because large numbers of people come to see it as a result of its connection to the book, it was moved to the Telfair Academy, a museum housing nineteenth and twentieth-century American and European art.

I arrived at The Gryphon Tea Room of the Savannah School of Art and Design, its walls covered with immense mahogany bookcases embellished with decorative details and filled with books. Sofas, easy chairs, and tables are arranged in conversation groups. There I took a pleasant cup of tea before heading for a quick peek at the Georgia State Railroad Museum, a museum to Victorian railroading with steam engines and roundhouse.

Two more houses were on my itinerary. The Green-Meldrin House is a stately Gothic Revival house in a manicured courtyard that seems to have tamed Nature, with large grey paving stones. Neo-gothic aprons from the porch ceilings mirror wrought iron railings below. Built in the 1850s by Charles Green, a cotton merchant and ship owner, it is now the property of St. John's Episcopal Church. The house was used as Sherman's headquarters during the Union Army's occupation of Savannah during the Civil War. According to the docent, use of his house was offered by Mr. Green in order to ensure that his house was spared destruction by the occupying army. In the Isaiah Davenport House the guide explained that an empire sofa was displayed with a large tear in its upholstery so that visitors could see how chairs were stuffed with horsehair and cotton in the nineteenth century.

I saved the Bonaventure Cemetery for the end of the trip. I journeyed to Savannah for this cemetery tour above all else—because of the reputation this garden of the Savannah marshland has for fun, quirkiness, and a little hocus-pocus. It has its share of extravagant Victorian mourning monuments; the Victorian period was an era when indulgence in bereavement had its little pleasures. The nineteenth-century cult of mourning received great encouragement from Queen Victoria, who never wished to leave off mourning, it seemed, and who corresponded with Mary Todd Lincoln about their shared fascination with grief and with trying to make contact with those in the Great Hereafter. Nineteenth-century funeral monuments are maudlin, oppressive by their very weight and mass, and by their large marble statuary. Stone angels are not ethereal and evocative of resurrection, but weighty and earthbound. Stone roses covering caskets are lovely and hard. Beautiful stone women in lamentation maintain a firm hold on the departed, keeping them in the ground rather than permitting their souls to take flight from the clay.

It seems a great deal of effort had gone into holding onto one's loved one, yet it happened from time to time someone was buried alive. People in catatonic or coma states would sometimes appear to be dead to people who had none of the sophisticated medical monitoring machines we rely on today, and sometimes unconscious people were interred. The tour guide brought to our attention a bell next to a mausoleum. He told us that when someone had been prematurely buried, she could pull the bell upon awakening to call for help; that circumstance, he explained, was the origin of the phrase "saved by the bell."

Gracie's Grave is a popular graveyard tourist destination. A pretty little girl sculpted in white marble, six year old Gracie died in 1889. Her family moved from Savannah and are buried in New England. She is alone behind a wrought-iron fence; a lush garden of tall, tightly-packed flowers with overhanging live oak surrounds her grave. People frequently leave her little gifts and watch for her ghost. Conrad Aiken's grave is marked by a bench instead of a headstone; the bench is inscribed: "Cosmos Mariner. Destination Unknown." The common explanation given out is that Aiken wished to encourage people to come to visit—even to party—on his grave. The tour guide told of us a mausoleum from which the multiple bodies in residence were stolen; he explained that Savannah has always been a center of Voodoo activity, and that since no one has ever recovered the bodies people assume they were taken by practitioners of that religion. Not only ghost hunters, but voodoo hunters and zombie hunters too, traipse around Bonaventure Cemetery, as do people like us in the tour group, who enjoy proximity to those macabre elements.

Bonaventure Cemetery is on the Savannah River, wild plants along its bank trying to re-assert their primacy. Beautiful though they are, live oaks encroach and hem in upon all sides. The flora adds to the unnerving vibrations one experiences when prowling around graveyards and old houses with sad histories. The preponderance of gorgeous and aggressive vegetation creates an uncanny feeling that the human wanderer is a trespasser in an alien world.

New Orleans Voodoo

New Orleans is French, exotic, Spanish, and macabre, brought forth from the bayou in 1718 when France was struggling to establish her Louisiana colony in the face of hurricanes, Indian attacks, and diseases spread by mosquitoes. Indentured servants were brought from Europe to provide a workforce; their offspring born in the inhospitable New World were *creoles (*a generic term for the French who were born in America). The meaning of the word *Creole* evolved after to incorporate the groups with whom the French intermarried and their descendants: Africans brought to the New World in slavery, Native Americans, French settlers from Canada (Arcadians) and Spanish settlers (after Louisiana was ceded to Spain following the Seven Years' War). No one of these cultural groups became dominant—rather, they combined into a non-homogenous (and nonpareil) societal gumbo. Partly because it is so hard to label, define or pigeonhole, New Orleans exudes an alluring mystique and a certain lawlessness inherent in its refusal to conform to a paradigm.

My exploration of the Louisiana delta began with a visit to the Oak Alley Plantation. Oak Alley is a mansion built in 1839 in nearby Vacherie and is famous for its avenue of live oaks that form a canopy over the drive approaching the house—the *allee*. Footage was shot here for *Hush Hush Sweet Charlotte* and *Interview with a Vampire* (it was Louis's home). At Oak Alley a docent welcomes her guests into the Big House with plenty of Southern hospitality. In the course of her tour she points out that the marble mantel at which the guests are looking is really painted wood, marble being difficult to obtain when the house was built. She explains that the architecture was adapted to the climate, open windows symmetrically aligned to allow breezes to blow in one side of the house and out the other in the days before air conditioning. In addition to seeing the mansion, guests can visit the Slave Quarters and explore exhibits on the history of sugar cane production, as well. Oak Alley was built when planters were becoming wealthy from sugar cane, cotton and tobacco, but its glory was fleeting and the plantation endured its share of misery. Its owner, Jaques Roman, died of tuberculosis in 1848. His family were unable to maintain the profitability of the enterprise and the plantation fell into disrepair. Oak Alley is said to contain still the restless spirits of those who suffered there—the slaves who built the house and worked the plantation and the family who owned it. *Ghost-Hunters* filmed a *Travel Channel* program here. Spirits are believed to be bound by their misery to this once-glorious relic of American aspiration to Old World aristocracy.

The bus that had taken me to Oak Alley on its return trip followed the Mississippi, taking River Road to New Orleans. On the way the bus stopped to allow passengers to walk up to the riverbank. I was amazed at the width of the Mississippi River: to know it is a big river and to see for oneself that it is a big river are two different things. It is wide and it is muddy—almost like a *café au lait* pudding. Large vessels navigate its thick and placid brown water.

In the evening following a magnificent gastronomic experience at *Antoine's* that included *Bananas Foster* and French champagne, I ended the day at Bourbon Street. Looking into the doorways of two or three liquor establishments, I stopped when I came to one that was pouring the most delicious Dixieland Jazz from out its doors. I took a seat and a cocktail while listening to the trombones and clarinets. Although I purchased a recording of the band, I was never able to enjoy it in the same way at home. The band led a parade, twisting around the bar and then down Bourbon Street, the parade getting longer and longer as people in the balconyed and wrought-ironed street joined the line. The line eventually dissolved into the mass of pedestrians, its boundaries disappearing. The intoxicating experience is not reproducible in a recording.

With chicory coffee and a *beignet* at Brennan's the next day was started, the culinary stimulants being preparatory to a day of shopping on Royal Street. Named for its Parisian cousin, *Rue Royale*, Royal Street starts at Canal Street and continues through the French Quarter. I had need of shopping for a practical reason: according to my research the average temperatures of New Orleans at that time of year ranged in the high fifties and I had packed woolens. The actual temperatures were in the seventies, necessitating a new wardrobe. I stepped up to the plate, entered the boutiques with pretty French names, and purchased an imported French dress and shoes. I christened the fluttery organza dress my *Blanche DuBois* dress. Whenever I wore it in years after I revived a little of my New Orleans adventure.

No longer perspiring, I could now enjoy the street artists, whose fantasy, landscape, and caricature works hang on the wrought iron fences of Jackson Square. Trumpet players make their horns sing for the donations dropped into their instrument cases by pedestrians. When I visited New Orleans I had not yet been to France, and the antique shops in Royal Street made a great impression upon me. These were not the antique stores to which I was accustomed back home with their twentieth-century "old" furniture. On Royal Street the stores proffer centuries-old gilt furnishings from the palaces of Europe. Although the settees and bibelots exceeded my budget, I found browsing in these shops quite the satisfying experience.

My retail explorations underwent a metamorphosis as French antiques gave way to amulets and herbs: I found myself in a Voodoo store. One look around convinced me that this was a venue for sincere practitioners and not just a tourist trap. As I crossed the threshold to enter the store, my skin drew attention to itself and my hair began to rise. I sensed electric air as I studied the merchandise:

candles, herbs, oils, powders, charms, *gris-gris* (amulets). The arousal I experienced was not a negative sensation—I had always enjoyed the macabre in books and film. The difference was that I *felt* what real occult practice is. It is my psychic sense that was responding to the environment.

Louisiana Voodoo was formed by the introduction of enslaved Africans into the French Catholic colony of Louisiana. The African Voodoo brought by the slaves was characterized by ancestor worship and amulets and charms (not curses and zombies). Practitioners readily absorbed the God and saints and prayers and music of the Catholic Church into their faith; they had no concept that the faiths were mutually exclusive. The French practice of slavery discouraged the breaking-up of families, and the slave population of Louisiana was able to develop its own culture in the slave quarters. Boundaries became blurred by interracial unions. The practice of Voodoo flourished in a region that appreciated good luck charms and protection spells to guard them against the threats of disease, natural disaster, and warfare with the displaced native people. The Voodoo King and Queen became powerful social figures for people of all shades of skin and all social classes. Louisiana Voodoo is still a living religion.

The tomb of Marie Laveau, a nineteenth-century Voodoo Queen, is frequented by both tourists and the faithful. During her lifetime large numbers of New Orleaners sought her out for help and advice, and thousands attended her St. John's Eve event in Bayou St. John. Her tomb in St. Louis Cemetery #1 is still a site where her followers come to Marie to request favors, by performing certain rituals upon her grave. For visitors from other places, the above-ground tombs of St. Louis Cemetery are spooky in their own right—little houses where the dead live above ground strike people very differently who are accustomed to burying the dead under the ground. The above-ground tombs are an innovation that was developed because of delta geology and the frequency of flooding—above-ground burial is more likely to maintain the dead *in* their coffins.

The two adventures remaining to this trip reinforced my sense of New Orleans exoticism and the wild independence of natural forces in the delta. With their paddle wheels splashing and steam puffing from their smoke stacks riverboats travel up and down the Mississippi River. A riverboat cruise on the Mississippi is a good way to feel the power of the flowing water beneath your feet. A conduit for European explorers plunging into the wilderness of the New World, for the conveyance of settlers, and for the conduct of trade, the Mississippi is a force harnessed by people who have asserted dominion over the environment. As if they own the river, the jazz musicians aboard the paddleboats stake their claim with blues and marches. Passengers dining below deck and promenading above capture pieces of New Orleans in their cameras. Beneath the boat the power of the flowing river abides. From time to time the Mississippi rebels, asserting the primacy of the earth and—despite earthworks and sandbags—the river rises over its banks, erasing the territorial claims of humans. New Orleans parties on the fringes of impending disaster.

The tangled nature of French-elegant city and the natural world impressed me once more as I enjoyed a boat ride through the bayou. As the boat drifts on water thickly green with floating vegetation, enclosed by cypress trees and Spanish moss, alligators swimming along-side the boat and long-beaked birds flying overhead—civilization seems very far away indeed. The bayou is an isolated and mysterious place. There is no solid land and no view of the horizon. The Mississippi delta is too wild to tame. Its watery paths of murky depths—thick with vegetation on, in, and overhanging the bayou—signal the unrelenting grasp that nature maintains on the city of New Orleans. Here, people seem organic extensions of nature, the offspring of highly demarcated French culture loosed upon a post-Edenic garden. Amphibious and winged things—alligators, snakes, turtles and birds—live here where people trespass.

From equal parts settlers of different cultures, Mississippi River, and murky swamp water, simmered in a cauldron and stirred by

168

tropical storm winds, emerged the Creole people who created for themselves a new society. In the new Creole social order taboos were challenged, races mixed, Church dogma absorbed into African Voodoo, convention and languages re-envisioned. Louisiana Voodoo is emblematic of a people who—leaving the constraints of civilization—went to the delta and brazenly confronted the natural and supernatural worlds in all their starkness in the swamps of the Mississippi.

Time Travel in Phoenix

The palatial marble lobby of the Phoenix, Arizona resort was the scene of nearly a thousand conventioneers directing their shiny brass luggage carts laden with pyramids of pink cartons and suitcases, preparing to scatter to their homes all over the world in the aftermath of the *National Barbie Collectors Convention.* I, however, was getting ready to embark upon a different kind of journey: I had arranged for a guide to drive me into the desert. Although the destinations on my itinerary that day would amount to only a few miles, my ultimate design was to travel more than half a millennium—*into the past.*

My driver helped me into his time machine—er, van—and drove me out into the American Southwest. I saw out my window the receding view of precision-manicured hotel landscaping that featured an assortment of cacti and other desert plants that are quite exotic to a Midwestern visitor. Spherical, mouse-eared, tentacled, or formed like hairy pompoms created for giant-size cheerleaders to shake, the succulent cacti blossom in the hard, dry dirt of the flower beds bounded by green turf moistened by irrigation water in the oasis-like resort.

We drove toward vast vistas of hills and mountains, arid and rocky, hard-edged with patches of prickly dry brush. Out here, away from modern concrete civilization, golf courses, and strip malls, saguaros grow wild, dotting the rough brown hills with points of green. They rise up above the scrub and reign over the little mouse-eared prickly cacti at their feet, who sport fluffy bonnets of white-petaled flowers. The hot, hazy sun bakes the air as it

170

climbs higher into the morning sky. My instinct was to scan the environment for shade, but the desert plants yield none, save for the tiniest of creatures.

We drove into the land of the Anasazi, ancient Native Americans whose unchronicled disappearance has spawned generations of theories that range from abduction by aliens harvesting earthlings to annihilation by cataclysmic ecological events. The name *Anasazi* is a word that refers to people who lived where water is scarce. Current scholarship suggests that the Anasazi did not "disappear," but migrated instead, southward as the rainfall totals lessened and the water table that sustained their corn-farming dried up, over an extensive dry period. The Anasazi were "prehistoric"—that is to say without a written record of their culture. Modern archaeologists qualify that label, though—they are learning to *read* the story of the Anasazi by other means—for there is more than one way to communicate a legacy.

To learn their story I visited *Montezuma's Castle*. It is a five-story edifice containing about twenty rooms, built of stone walls bound by red clay and mud along the side of a limestone cliff. Erected circa 1200–1450 A.D., the curve of the building follows the arc of the recess into which it is built. Its floors are made of crisscrossed layers of logs covered with woven mats and topped by a compound of mud and clay. The name by which we know it was given it by early sixteenth-century European explorers who erroneously thought the site was related to the Aztec ruler Montezuma. It is situated about 100 feet above the base of the cliff, high above where the Beaver Creek flows and floods annually. The guide explained that the people who built *Montezuma's Castle* had to hoist the stones from the ground to the height at which the building was being constructed, and that the lofty complex was reached by means of ladders. The T-shaped doors and windows, pottery, and feathers link *Montezuma's Castle* to the Anasazi, while other artifacts indicate a mingling of different cultures by trade.

Smaller holes dot the expanse of the cliffs. These were the

granaries, storage chambers for maize and other provisions that needed to be protected from damp, predators, and thieves. Condominium complexes such as *Montezuma's Castle* functioned as both city and fortification, the height serving a defensive function. *Montezuma's Castle* was abandoned circa 1450 A.D. The ruins having been ransacked by tourists and pot hunters, in 1951 access to the interior was restricted by the National Park Service.

Archaeologists use forensic clues to demonstrate that the Anasazi did not merely dematerialize. They have been tracking the migration of the Anasazi by the movement of their pottery, as their northern style moved southward and into Mexico. Their funerary customs also followed a southward path, northern burial practices coming into contact with southern cremation rites. The evidence indicates that theirs was not a peaceful migration; hence, the defensive constructions of cliff-dwellings. Traumatized skeletal remains tell forensic stories of warfare. There is even evidence of ritual cannibalism found in the remains of tortured and ritually dismembered human sacrifices, who were baked and roasted.

The Anasazi were dry-land farmers who learned to grown corn about 1000 B.C. in the Four Corners region where Colorado, Utah, Arizona, and New Mexico converge in the desert. As rainfall decreased and the water table fell, the rain-god worshiping people of the north moved south to find a suitable location to cultivate the maize that was the staple of their diet, reaching Mexico by the fifteenth century A.D.

They brought their culture with them. The *greathouse* served as a ceremonial venue, a multi-story building constructed around a *kiva*. *Great kivas* are depressions dug into the ground, circular and aligned with the celestial movements; they were used for rituals to propitiate the nature gods. Private homes have smaller kivas for familial use. Holes in the kivas are thought to represent a passage from this world to the next; called *sipapu*, they indicate the subterranean water that sustains life in the desert. Archaeologists propose that many kivas were destroyed by ritual burning—burning that was clearly purposeful and not accidental—as the Anasazi vacated them on their migration.

Many theories have been put forth in an attempt to interpret the rock art found in Anasazi caves. Rock art consists of *petroglyphs* (etchings in the rock) and *pictographs* (paintings on the rock) of the cave walls. Anthropologists are trying to reconstruct an Anasazi mythology from their rock art depictions of shield and spear-wielding stylized human figures, spirals, and animals—and animals walking on spirals. Some people see the spirals as representative of an inward, shamanistic journey. Others hypothesize they are related to the underworld or the next life. Some suggest that they indicate contact with aliens from outer space.

Other features of the Anasazi culture that moved south include the erection of aviaries and the ritual use of feathers. Turkeys were ritualistically beheaded and sacrificed, and their feathers were used for making blankets and robes. The Anasazi engaged in a large export business in turkey feathers traded to southern markets. The T-shaped doors and windows are linked by many researchers to the Mesoamerican rain god Tlaloc; the T-shape in the Mayan language means "wind" or "breath of life."

Tuzigoot was the next stop in my time-traveling exploration of the ancient Southwest. It is a pueblo ruin near Clarkdale, Arizona that was built circa 1000–1400 A.D. *Tuzigoot* is laid out on a site approximately 500 by 100 feet in area, with both interior and exterior stone masonry walls. It was built to conform to the terrain of the promontory. Foundations and partial walls of a two-to-three story building survive. *Tuzigoot* once had over one hundred rooms. Although a modern staircase now joins the levels, when the Anasazi lived there they used ladders between the floors. I rambled all over, willing the stones to talk to me, and looking at the surrounding mountains in the distance, noting the relative greenness of the land here. *Tuzigoot* is located in the Verde Valley, where the occasional flooding of the Verde River facilitates a greater presence of vegetation. Still extant are some remains of a signal system on the promontories that enabled communication among a series of pueblo communities like *Tuzigoot* that the Anasazi constructed in the Verde Valley, along the route of the river.

A few clumps of grasses are growing up among the skeletal remains of *Tuzigoot*. When I visited, the site was covered with insects that looked like flying ants, which I attempted to disregard as I walked through the stones, trying to imagine the life of an Anasazi in the large pueblo community. In the museum are housed artifacts retrieved from the site. Until the Anasazi civilization collapsed in the fifteenth century, this was a bustling center along a river valley trade route. Like *Montezuma's Castle, Tuzigoot* was abandoned about 1450 A.D.

Following *Tuzigoot*, I headed to the *Copper Art Museum*, a wonderful collection of copper art and other copper products from all over the world. I asked the docent who did all the polishing, and I was astounded to learn that none was needed in the arid clime of Arizona (In my damp part of the world, one wages a continual war against rust and tarnish). Copper walls and ceilings, boilers, lamps, pots, plates, and jewelry are among the many artifacts gathered in the warmly glowing collection that demonstrates the many uses for this metal mined in Arizona. It was time to board the nearby *Verde Canyon Railroad*. Formerly a mining railroad, it now operates as a scenic ride in the canyon. Nestled deep in the cleft of the grey and brown rocky mountains, the train threads the valley, carrying passengers over trestles and through pitch-black tunnels, chugging along the edge of the mountain. At the base of the hard rock crags, trees and other flora thrive on the moist banks of the Verde River. Here is the source of life. It is no wonder that the Anasazi revered rain and water—scarcity of water in their lives was death. As long-term dry periods influenced water table levels, the dry-land farmers needed to relocate toward other sources of the life-giving liquid. My guide said that even today outlying people need to have their water trucked in.

The train ride is a pleasant excursion providing a magnificent view of the mountains and valley. I had the good fortune to sit by a man who operated a tour company and who practiced Wicca; we enjoyed exchanging anecdotes about Salem and things magical. As I traveled the valley by train I was considering also the people who had lived here, who had traveled on foot and who farmed for subsistence with stone tools, who had to learn to adapt their agriculture to floods and droughts, who had to follow the water. They had to pack up their portable goods, move their communities, and then settle down again further south. They had to move into land already inhabited by other people.

Driving back toward Phoenix from the Verde Valley, I stopped to eat dinner at a mountain-top restaurant, behind which was a terraced garden. Steppes roughly quadrilateral were sculpted along the rocky slope of the hillside. These were enclosed by retaining walls of stones to prevent the erosion of soil down the hill in the rain. I had encountered steppe farming once before, when I walked up the winding roads of the olive gardens in Sorrento, Italy. People have always had to adapt to the earth—our home and the source of our life.

Modern city-dwelling people often feel disconnected, separate from nature—until cataclysmic events disrupt their lives, until hurricanes tear down retaining walls and rivers burst dams, or until the ground breaks open beneath their feet; yet, many people the world over still dwell where their feet touch the ground, and where soil, plants, and animals surround their homes. Like the Anasazi, these people may have a greater awareness of our connectedness with the rest of nature—and of the power of natural forces to sustain or destroy us.

Meditation on the tremendous power of nature can produce a sense of awe. In our time, the worship of nature and sacrifice to the gods thereof may seem a macabre kind of mythology—an uneducated approach to geology, physics, or astronomy—but to an Anasazi woman or man who looked to the god who provided life-giving water in a hot, dusty world, who offered sacrifices of turkeys and people through rituals to please the giver of life, awe in the presence of the source of life was a deeply-held faith. The sublime experience that enables a person to feel awe is a profound personal encounter between a soul and the cosmos. It is a glimpse into the boundless and a hint of our relation to it. One person's religion is another's superstition. Each person, however, attempts to make sense of himself in the universe, whether ancient Anasazi or curious contemporary traveler.

Mexican Macabre

Tequila and Skeletons

I went to California for the National Barbie Collectors' Convention, the third of six I have attended. The annual convention is quite a big shebang hosted jointly by Mattel and local Barbie fan clubs, and it hops from city to city. The theme that year was "Barbie's Grand Tour"—it was my favorite convention, for I love traveling as much as Barbie does. I was excited to find myself in Orange County, California among the palm trees. I posed for one photo next to a Barbie-pink Fiat, and for another wearing a white sequined evening gown (for the *White Nights in St. Petersburg* gala) by the pool under the palm trees—and I felt quite the Hollywood starlet. I greedily photographed the extensive dioramas of Barbie in Russia boarding the Siberian Railroad, Barbie in London at William and Kate's wedding, and Barbie in Paris at an atelier and at the entrance to the *Metropolitain*. I bought some vintage girls for my collection and wined and dined away several days of banquets, fashion shows, stage entertainments, and collectors' workshops. I met designers from Barbie's early years and the present time. The convention concluded with the unveiling of that year's exclusive convention doll, designed by *Magia 2000*.

The next day I headed for Hollywood. In an open-air tourist car I rode down Sunset Boulevard to Beverly Hills, where the guide pointed out Greystone Manor (the Collinwood mansion in the 1991 revival series of television's *Dark Shadows*), and I elatedly snapped a quick photo. I was on a camera safari, looking for big game. I snapped Tom Cruise's house, George Gershwin's too, and a house where Madonna used to live. I snared W.C. Fields's, Peter

Falk's, Gene Kelly's, Lucille Ball's, and Paul Newman's and Joanne Woodward's houses. I sighted live game in my lens: I shot my camera point-blank at a smiling and waving Larry King, who was on the sidewalk in front of his house. I oh-too-briefly visited Rodeo Drive, and then I took a picture of the Hollywood sign, ending the journey at Grauman's Chinese Theater. I bought a Hollywood Hard Rock shirt and walked the sidewalks, photographing the hand-printed stars of Steven Spielberg, William Shatner, Elton John, and Jack Nicholson. I posed with Lucille Ball, Rambo, and Michael Jackson on Hollywood Boulevard for tips—and after an exciting day returned to my Orange County lair.

The second day following the convention I traveled by bus from Orange County to Tijuana. The bus took me past San Diego, along Highway 5, hugging the coast of the Pacific Ocean on my right. It is a coast green with low brush and short bushes. The ocean was a light blue close to the land that morning and a deeper blue toward the horizon, and the water was calmly rippling. The sky was a milky blue, haze between the sun and me. On my left were hills, scruffy with a green brush coat that was brown in large patches.

Approaching the United States/Mexico border I could see hills covered now with tightly-packed concrete boxes in the distance beyond the border checkpoint, a dry, thirsty-looking vista. The sun shone through the haze and bounced back off the concrete. The bus came to a stop and the driver instructed his passengers to disembark and cross over the pedestrian bridge on foot at the San Ysidro border crossing: he said it would involve much less red tape than taking the bus over the border. While on the bus I had struck up a conversation with a couple of Australian nurses who were on a grand tour of the United States. At the border they obliged me by taking my picture near the sign that read: "*Limite de Los Estades Unidos dos Mexicanos.*" I was looking around at the high chain-link fences surrounding the checkpoint and ensuring that traffic was flowing in only one direction, when the driver encouraged everyone to hustle and reminded the passengers what time to be back at the border. I joined the mass of people walking up the steep bridge that was hemmed in by tall, wire mesh sides that prevented people from jumping or falling off. From the apex of the pedestrian bridge I saw the green, white and red flag of Mexico flapping in the breeze ahead of me.

Hundreds of people walked down the declining slope and were processed through customs, coming out of the booths into a concrete street of concrete-cube buildings. Some were painted yellow, but most grey. Most were unadorned boxes, while here and there were highly detailed decorative wrought iron balcony railings. Most windows were barred. In the distance I could see dry dirt hills with green brush.

The driver guided his passengers to the *gringo-friendly* (English-speaking) tourist center on Avenida Revolucion. I felt like Dorothy going from black-and-white Kansas into Technicolor Oz. The sun still beat upon grey concrete streets, but the buildings there are painted bright primary color shades of yellow, red, blue, and green. Palm trees line the streets, and outdoor tables and chairs are set out in front of the restaurants.

Blocks of stalls display brightly-hued t-shirts in pink and purple and blue, red, and yellow which feature Aztec motifs and skulls and skeletons. In this street decorative wrought iron is plentiful and cacti in large clay pots dot the sidewalks between the palms. Colorful umbrellas shade the sellers in the stalls, and everyone calls out a welcome to the *Senorita* as she walks by. TJ Pharmacy has an open store front where a mannequin in a clichéd sexy nurse uniform greets customers in the doorway and a large-print placard details the pharmaceuticals for sale with no prescription needed here that would require a prescription in the U.S.—from antibiotics to Cialis. I met up again with the Australian nurses who were now wearing sombreros, and we had our picture taken together. Then I ate a delicious taco dinner at an umbrella table at a restaurant that sported a sign reading, *Say No to Drugs. Say Yes to Tacos.*

I went shopping in all the flamboyantly-colored stores piled high with souvenirs—from *serapes* to silver jewelry to tequila. In each store I entered the clerk offered me a shot of tequila—and pressed me to accept more. Browsing for souvenirs, I noted quite a few Virgin Mary's and angels of painted wood or of ceramic, and a lot of Aztec Quetzalcoatls and other Mesoamerican deities. A plethora of *calaveras* (skulls) and *calacas* (skeletons) were jumbled among them. In Tijuana every day is *Dia de los Muertos*, it seems. Skull art abounds here, on the shelves of the stores and on the t-shirts. In some stores I saw *offrendas* (altars for the deceased) with photographs, memorabilia, and food offerings. Skulls of sugar candy were brightly colored. Skeletons in wood, metal, and ceramic—just about every medium conceivable—were among the wares that ranged from cheap souvenirs to fine art.

Dia de los Muertos is a Mexican holiday celebrated October 31–November 2. It is a fusion of a thousands of years-old tradition of homage to the dead dating back to the ancient Aztecs and the Catholicism imposed upon the indigenous people of Mexico by the Spanish Conquistadores. The Catholic All Hallows' Eve and All Saints' and All Souls' Days merge with more ancient celebrations into *Dia de los Muertos*. Rather than fearing the dead, observers celebrate the lives of those gone forward. Some spend the night at their graves conversing with their friends who have gone the next step in the journey. People hope to maintain contact with the dead. They do not employ occult ceremonies, séances, and Ouija boards; they simply say, "*Hola, Jose,*" and resume where they had left off, sharing food and drink and conversation.

It was June, but in Tijuana it felt very much like *Dia de los Muertos*. I purchased some of the decorative skulls and one interesting hybridization—several small *calaveras* inside a brightly painted blue wooden cross. The dead do not seem very far removed from the living in a town where a shrine to the Virgin Mary (a statue of a dark-haired Virgin wearing a red robe inside a little blue house covered with flowers, the glass doors in front secured with iron bars) is a block away from an automobile-sized head of

Montezuma. Skeletal *La Calavera Catrinas*—skulls wearing great European-style hats with big plumes—laugh at the amalgam of faiths. What is is what is. The soul after death is what it is, despite the catechisms of competing faiths. And here, in the land of *Dia de los Muertos*, death is not so dreadful, nor are the dead.

It was time to go. As I hastened back to the pedestrian bridge and the slow customs process I looked back at the stark grey part of Tijuana beyond the Avenida Revolucion. A three-story green box building with a red tile roof was topped with a sign that read "*Hospital Mexico*," the width of its frontage held six parking spaces. Tijuana is a big city, and I saw only a small part of it. Soon after, the United States Department of State was warning U.S. citizens to avoid that part of Mexico because of increasing activity of drug cartels. I had been to Mexico before—to Chichen Itza and Tulum on the once-Mayan Atlantic side of our neighbor to the South. I listened to the story the Mexicans wished to tell in the short time I had to hear it, the story of a proud people who had had to shoulder the invasions of European colonial governments, American Manifest Destiny, and drug lords.

The next day was my final day in California. I walked from the hotel to Disneyland—and my first stop was *Sleeping Beauty's Castle* where I felt five years old once more. My heart leapt at the sight of the gilt pink and blue conical towers, their triangular pennants waving in the breeze. I visited *Snow White's Scary Adventure* and the lair of the jealous wicked witch who poisoned the apple. I rode the *Alice in Wonderland* caterpillar, swirled in the teacups, and worked off my *Blue Bayou* lunch in *Tarzan's Treehouse*. I ended up with two creepy attractions: the *Twilight Zone*-themed *Hollywood Tower*, full of ghostly specters and poltergeist bustle, and then finally the *Haunted Mansion*.

In *The Hollywood Tower*, elevator doors close and open to scary scenes reminiscent of the long corridors where malevolent ghosts appeared in *The Shining*, as the ride took me higher and higher in preparation for the big drop (that I had not known was coming!).

The *Haunted Mansion* was my first encounter with holograms, which are really surprisingly lifelike and three-dimensional. The mansion is a New Orleans-style pillared and corniced French Quarter mansion with two stories of wrought-iron trimmed veranda and balconies. Inside candelabra are festooned with cobwebs. A casket nearly buried beneath funeral floral arrangements creeks open, as skeletal fingers push up the lid. Ghosts pop out and shriek and elicit screams and giggles from the passengers aboard the cars.

The dead are rendered very differently in Disneyland and in Tijuana—in Disneyland they are feared. Ghosts and paranormal phenomena are threatening. North of the border, spirits are exorcised and people seek protection from the unwelcome dead. South of the border they are invited to sit and stay awhile. The last two days of my California holiday left me poised on the fulcrum of competing ideologies regarding the spirit realm and its relation to the living.

Man-Eating Gods of the Yucatan

The irresistible dark mystery of the pre-Columbian Yucatan peninsula was what beckoned me to Mexico. To this end I booked a hotel in Cancun, which was to be my jumping-off place for an exploration of the eerie secrets of the people who used to live there. The balcony of my Caribbean-facing room afforded a lovely view of melded blue sky and sea, white foaming waves rolling onto the sand. On the beach was a wooden lifeguard hut that was covered by a thatched roof, on top of which was another thatched-roof hut in miniature, seemingly reached by the ladder leaning against its wall. Further from shore the sun was reflected by the water in many bright points of light as by a thousand shards of a broken mirror. I regarded the view from the balcony, the Caribbean breeze whipping my skirt up parachute-like, and then I went inside to change into a bathing suit. For a time I frolicked in the waves, and I purchased silver bracelets from a peddler on the beach. Sunbathing was a doomed experiment for me—there was much too much to do to stay still very long. I shopped and enjoyed *real* Mexican food, and even made a shaky attempt at snorkeling before the day was out.

The next morning I boarded a tour bus to leave behind the sunshiny beach resort and to enter the shadowy and dense jungle. The forest road was very narrow and the vegetation lush so that the horizon and the sky were obscured from view by the tall trees growing high on both sides of the road. As the guide maintained a steady stream of information about the Yucatan, I was looking at huts alongside the road, their roofs thatched with banana leaves. From these banana leaf roofs arose television antennae, and in front

184

of these huts were stacked Coca-Cola crates. I asked the driver whether the people with television access were satisfied with their lifestyle, and he said they were "content."

As the bus emerged from the jungle into a clearing, stone buildings in varying states of disrepair came into view. Barefoot children stood in the dirt road before open doorways above which billboards displayed pictures of the sandy beaches I had left behind. The bus was approaching Chichen Itza. I had come to Mexico to explore the civilization of the Maya by visiting its sepulchral cities.

The Maya have lived in southeastern Mexico and Central America since around 2000 B.C., where they flourished until the conquest by Spain in the sixteenth and seventeenth centuries A.D. The ancient Maya were a society of city-states whose relations were characterized by shifting alliances as they competed for control of trade routes and resources. Commerce was conducted throughout Mexico and as far away as Guatemala, over land and by canoe along the rivers and coastline of Mesoamerica. Not possessing the wheel, nor having yet domesticated pack animals, the Maya employed human power to move the commodities they were trading—obsidian, gold, cacao, textiles, and slaves (the slaves were primarily prisoners of war)—and to construct their great cities.

Early Mayan beliefs had been largely based on ancestor worship and shamanism and over time evolved into a cosmology that included a pantheon of gods whose functions and influences were rather labile. Divine mood was dependent upon the positions of the celestial bodies, and the king was the mediator between the gods and the human race. By means of ceremonies based upon astronomical and astrological calculation the king sought to placate the gods. Mayan architecture was designed for the purpose of tracking the course of the sun, Venus and the other planets, and the stars—and the highly accurate Mayan calendar was based upon the regular movement of the heavenly bodies. Based on their foreknowledge of planetary positions and the movements of the stars, the Mayan people could anticipate what the gods would be wanting from them in time to appease them and to forestall their wrath. The Mayan mythology was a complex belief system that included thirteen vertical levels of heavens above and nine below the world, as well as the relative positions of the east, west, north and south, each with its own properties.

El Castillo (The Castle) arose before me in the distance as the bus approached Chichen Itza. The stone-block pyramid is ninety-eight feet high, and on each of its four sides is a flight of stairs leading up to the twenty-foot high rectangular structure on the flat summit of the pyramid: the Temple. Until renamed by the Spanish Conquistadores, *El Castillo* had been known as the Temple of Kukulkan, the Feathered Serpent. It used to preside over a large and bustling pre-Columbian city. Feathered Serpent deities sit open-mouthed—hungrily awaiting sacrificial offerings—at the bases of the stairs. Carvings cover the walls of the buildings in this ancient city, carvings of gods and kings, warriors and sacrificial victims, which at one time had been painted in vibrant colors that have since eroded away. I scrambled—at first—and then carefully picked my way to the top. The stairs were very steep and the steps shallow, so that I had to place my feet carefully to ensure an adequate foothold. The *chac-mool* arrested my attention at the top—a reclining stone figure of a man with bent knees and head facing outward from the pyramid, its stomach flat to receive a sacrifice. It was a sacrificial altar.

The Mayan gods are bloodthirsty, and sacrifices were prepared for them by an assortment of rituals and for various occasions: the erection of a new edifice, the crowning of a king, or the start of a military campaign. Decapitation and extraction of the heart from a living person were the most common methods of preparing the sacrifice. Distinguished enemy captives—warriors and kings—were the best food of the gods. Some sacrificial victims were sealed alive in tombs; others were killed by a rite of slowly shooting arrows into them or by disembowelment. Torture usually preceded death, and the greater the occasion the more extreme was the ritual torture.

Numerous relics bear witness to the blood tribute the Maya paid their cruel heavenly overlords. At Chichen Itza there is a Sacred Cenote, a well, a natural sinkhole. The Yucatan has a number of these above the underground rivers. The Maya linked sinkholes to the rain god, and they made pilgrimages to them. Sacrificial victims were often tossed alive into these near-bottomless pits. Still today skeletons of tortured sacrificial victims, as well as precious objects, can be found in the cenotes.

The Great Ball Court is one of thirteen ball courts at Chichen Itza. Approximately 550 feet by 230, it is a grassy enclosure surrounded by highly sculpted walls. On the east side of the enclosure is the Temple of the Jaguar, and other temples are on the north and south sides. Depictions of decapitated players are sculpted on the interior walls, blood spurting out from their necks in the form of stylized serpents. The balls used in the Ballgame were sometimes the sacrificial victims themselves, trussed up into balls. The sacrificial victims were the finest ballgame players, who were after the game tortured and decapitated.

De Los Craneos (The Platform of the Skulls) features four rows of Death's Head carvings. It is one of several extant platforms dedicated to the veneration of the bloodthirsty Mesoamerican divinities which have survived the centuries at Chichen Itza. Also among these are the Platform of the Eagles and Jaguars and the Platform of Venus.

Another pyramid still stands at Chichen Itza—*El Templode Los Guerreros y Mil Columnas* (Temple of the Warriors and the Thousand Columns). Atop the three-step pyramid are two rectangular structures, and a *chac-mool* sits on the top at the entrance to the temple. Surrounding the pyramid is a mass of columns, and even though the roofs that were once supported by the columns have long since vanished, several small buildings still endure at one end of the complex. The columns are richly carved with depictions of warriors and gods. As Chichen Itza is too extensive to be seen thoroughly in a single day, there were some buildings I did not have the opportunity to visit; these include a smaller *castillo*-type pyramid, the Osario whose temple-top is in ruins; *Le Iglesia*, a late-Mayan administrative building; and *El Caracol*, an observatory. There is a steam bath, too.

Finding myself back in Cancun after a day in the jungle of the *chac-mools* was a bit bewildering. The music-filled nightlife was in full swing. I had journeyed from the realm of the dead back to the land of the living. Torture and blood sacrifice were not on the minds of the people who filled the restaurant at which I indulged in a late dinner, enjoying the warm evening breeze under the stars.

I returned to the realm of the ancient Maya the next day, taking another excursion bus—this time to Tulum, the ancient walled city on the cliffs of the Yucatan Peninsula. Both fortress and important commercial center, the thick walls of the city protected its landward side; watch towers set along the walls resemble those of the medieval cities of Europe. From the thirteenth through the sixteenth centuries A.D. Tulum had been an important economic hub—trading with Guatemala over 400 miles away for obsidian and with Mexico for gold—until disease brought by the Spanish decimated the population in under one hundred years from their arrival. Now jungle is grown up around Tulum's skeletal remains. Lots of foundations and walls linger, as well as columns that no long support ceilings.

Several edifices still stand. The Temple of the Descending God is a one-room structure containing a sculpture of a winged figure that is a recurring motif in Tulum. The *Templo Dios Del Viento* (God of Winds Temple) is on the edge of a cliff. *El Castillo* is a temple overlooking the sea. The *Templo de los Frescoes* is a rectangular stone block structure on top of a larger rectangular base with columns. It is aligned with the progress the sun makes daily through the sky. Scrubby grounds with large swaths of sand form the floor of this jungle-cleared dead city. As I climbed on the *Templo de los Frescoes,* I tried to imagine what Tulum was like when it was full of Mayan people who looked at the world in such a different way than I do, unaware of the coming terminal plagues of Spanish weaponry and microbes.

While Mayan carvings are still telling their history through pictures and pictograms, only three coda survive, and a fourth text of dubious authenticity. Little remains to communicate their stories but mute great monuments and archaeological artifacts, for the Spanish burnt thousands of Mayan books. Whatever ancient Mayans' daily lives were, they must have lived beneath a somber shadow hovering over their world. The lords of the Mayan universe exalted in torture and gore—demanded fealty in human blood. They threatened famine and war, cataclysmic punishment should they not be appeased. In response, the Maya developed a machinery for feeding the gods their fellow men and women. As I contemplated the remains of the once pulsating city, I mused whether some ancient Mayan author had written a book about his Mayan world view, or perhaps whether there were any people who had imagined a different kind of society. Were there free-thinkers or dissenters or dreamers among the ancient Maya, and did they once leave a written record? It is nice to imagine one such text has survived the Spanish fires and is waiting to speak to us about lives lived under the control of man-devouring gods.

CHINESE MACABRE

Metropolises of the Living and of the Dead

Today China is officially atheist: the communist government has decreed that there is no spirit realm, and it has instituted a cult of the Communist Party and of the Party leaders. Yet, for at least 3,000 years before the conception of communism, Chinese leaders had been preoccupied with preparations for an afterlife—preparations at least as elaborate as those of the ancient Egyptians. Centuries of Chinese rulers have left behind funerary monuments and tombs whose chief message seems to be that they would, indeed, *take it with them*—their power, their possessions, and their armies. Historically, Chinese mythology has not been character-ized by a uniform system of beliefs: the mythology has varied by place and time, different myths having developed independently of one another. Nevertheless, throughout three thousand years of recorded history there has been a mythology that is dually focused on the earthly life and the afterlife, more recently integrating the teachings of Buddhism and Christianity into their ancestral belief systems.

I visited China with an escorted tour company. After arriving at the Beijing airport tourists gathered together at the Kempinski Hotel, where we would spend the first leg of our journey. The Kempinski is a modern, western-style luxury hotel. It has a beau-tiful indoor pool and tea garden. The sumptuous breakfast buffet included traditional Chinese, American, and European breakfast foods. Unfortunately, it was also the only time of day I might obtain coffee and bread over the weeks I traveled in China, a minor hardship for me, despite the excellence of the Chinese cuisine. The

191

hotel provided Western publications in the gift shop and internet for guests, which were not available for most Chinese citizens.

Whether home or abroad I begin most days with a walk of an hour or two, and I did so in Beijing. That is how I learned that the stories one hears of air pollution in Beijing are not exaggerated. Many pedestrians and cyclists were wearing face masks, understandably, for I felt as if I were walking behind the exhaust of a car as I treaded the sidewalk before dawn. The sidewalks and streets were very crowded at that time of day—rush hour. Some cars, but mostly hundreds (or even thousands) of bicycles, filled the streets. Women in business suits and dress shoes rode next to men carrying pyramids of boxes on their bicycle fenders, pyramids bigger than the bicycles themselves. One man rode past me with a pig sliced in half the long way on the back of his bicycle. People walked quickly along the sidewalks, some buying fast-food breakfasts—pancake-wrapped food sold by vendors manning grills in the storefronts. I noted many KFC and pizza restaurants; just about everything was available on pizza crusts.

The guide escorted our group by bus to the landmarks on our itinerary, and the Forbidden City was one of the highlights. The guide told us that there were nearly a thousand buildings here on about two hundred acres. The Forbidden City was constructed in the first quarter of the fifteenth century and was the location of the courts of the Ming and Qing dynasties. (Responding to our questions, the guide made an interesting aside: he said that in the past he had been required to submit tourists' questions to his superior, who would give him the answers the following day; now, he said, things were more liberal and he could answer questions himself.) Over the centuries the Forbidden City has undergone many expansions, and it experienced some damage during regime changes (including the Boxer Rebellion) and wars with foreign powers (i.e. the nineteenth-century Opium Wars and the Japanese Invasion of 1933). Until the last emperor, Puyi, abdicated in 1912, all of the emperors had lived here for half a millennium.

A moat and a twenty-eight foot wide by twenty-six foot tall Wall surrounds the city. There is a gate on each of the four sides. The Meridian Gate leads to the Imperial Way, on which (with a few exceptions) only the Emperor could walk. Each corner of the wall has a triple-eaved square turret with elaborate architectural details. The three great halls of the Outer Court (the Hall of Supreme Harmony, the Hall of Complete Harmony, and the Hall of Preserving Harmony) were used for public ceremonies, and the buildings of the Inner Court served as private quarters and offices of the Emperor. The buildings feature double roofs with yellow curved tiles (yellow is the color of the Emperor) decorated with phoenix, lion and dragon sculptures in the corners. The façades of the wooden buildings are painted in bright lacquers of primarily red, with intricate details in blue, green, and yellow. Red lattices cover the windows, and red doors are studded with golden nails. Ceilings are constructed of caissons with recessed panels or otherwise intricate arrangements of the highly-ornamented wood panels in the same colors of red, blue, green, and yellow. The interiors of the buildings hold treasures of tasseled lanterns, antiques both Chinese and European, gilded carved lions, porcelains and jades, and palace furnishings.

A nearly seven-acre stone courtyard lies before the Hall of Supreme Harmony. The far side of the square is bounded by the Golden Water River, a man-made waterway spanned by five marble bridges. The opposite side of the square ends at the three-tiered marble terrace before the Hall of Supreme Harmony. Two carved marble staircases flank a marble ramp carved in a bas-relief motif of dragons and phoenixes. Only the Emperor was permitted to walk on the ramp. Dragonhead water spouts ornament the marble balustrade. There are Imperial Gardens—but one cannot see all of this city of almost ten thousand rooms in one day.

Another excursion was to the Summer Palace which originated in 1152, the time of the Jin dynasty. A water reservoir was constructed, and palaces with lakes and gardens, in the Fragrant Hills on the outskirts of Beijing. The complex was not a permanent residence, functioning instead as a vast pleasure garden. By the nineteenth century it was in disrepair, until Empress Dowager Cixi redirected money from the military budget to restore the Summer Palace. After the abdication of Emperor Puyi the palace became a public park. Double-eaved curved tile roofs of the marble buildings rise above lush watery vegetation. Peacocks, lion and dragon sculptures add to the natural beauty. A marble boat sits in the lake—a delicate two-story marble palace aboard a marble barge. Along the Long Corridor from the Hall of Joy and Longevity to Shizhang Pavilion musicians sit on the rails playing music. A woman wearing a four-crowned hat with a pompom on top and a crocheted poncho was playing a stringed instrument I had never seen before, with a violin-type bow (a *jinghu*); further down the walkway I spied a man in a cap with a visor and a suit resembling a military or band uniform playing one, too. The Pavilion of Precious Clouds is a series of double-roofed buildings set into the ascending hill, and it really does resemble clouds floating up the hillside.

Another temple we visited was the Temple of Heaven, a complex built by the Ming and Qing dynasties in the fifteenth century and expanded in the sixteenth. Neglect and military occupations during the nineteenth century Second Opium War and Boxer Rebellion resulted in significant damage. Fully restored now, the Temple of Heaven features the Hall of Prayer for Good Harvests, a three-roofed circular building on a round triple-tiered marble base. Here the Emperor, as Son of Heaven, would offer sacrifice for good harvests. The architecture is designed for reverberation and multiplication of sound and prayer: the circular Imperial Vault of Heaven is surrounded by a marble Echo Wall, and the Circular Mound Altar is surrounded by a rail. In Chinese symbology, earth is square and heaven circular. Among the structures of the temple complex milled tourists and head-shaven monks in long grey and brown caftans. Magnificent topiaries of yellow flowers bursting from gigantic red fruits (reminding me of Bosch's *Garden of Earthly*

Delights) were mixed with vertical floral sculptures composed of rings of yellow flowers around red poles. The avenues were lined with towering fir trees. People can walk all over and touch these temple complexes in Beijing.

I was able to spend time among the living streets of present-day Beijing, which churns with activity. Modern glass high-rises dot city streets lined with concrete box buildings. People in western-style dress, wearing vests and jackets (the days were cool), park their basketed bicycles on crowded racks and socialize in small groups or play checkers. In the traditional markets colorful flags flutter over pedestrian concourses and all kinds of animals are sold for food in the grocers' stalls. Young men sit on curbs offering tiger pelts and other animals' furs for sale. In another part of Beijing near the hotel I located a western-style shopping mall featuring Chinese-designed fashions, and that is where I did my shopping. One of the restaurants that I enjoyed in Beijing, and which was similar to restaurants in the United States (as were all those which we frequented as a group), had one exotic difference. The difference at this one was that the toilets in the ladies' room stalls were built into the floor—there were no raised seats—necessitating a squatting posture (the other places we had visited had had western-style fixtures). The bathroom was beautiful, though, with mosaic tiles and floral arrangements.

On the way to Tiananmen Square the guide told us about the national bird, the crane—as in construction crane—proudly pointing out all the building going on around us in Beijing. When we reached Tiananmen he explained that the people greeting the bus were "Dollar People," who called, "Dollar, dollar," as they hawked souvenirs to tourists. Tiananmen Square is joined to the Forbidden City via the Tiananmen Gate (Gate of Heavenly Peace). The Mausoleum of Mao Zedong is here, as well as the National Museum of China and a People's Heroes Monument and People's Hall. The Monument to the People's Heroes is a stirring, robust sculptural group that evinces energy, strength, and determination; the figures hold guns aloft and strain muscles in attitudes of striving, pushing, and forging against an unnamed foe. The seventeenth-century stone square was enlarged to its massive size in the 1950s when it provided the stage for Soviet-style military parades celebrating the anniversaries of the People's Republic of China—and for the massacre of the student protesters in 1989. Today it is heavily policed and surveiled. When I was there in 2005 a sign was counting down the days until the 2008 Olympics, which were to be held in China. Soldiers in green uniforms with yellow stripes and red epaulettes marched in formation. A gigantic portrait of Mao Zedong looked down as students approached me and asked if they could please practice speaking English with me.

One evening we enjoyed a performance of the Beijing Opera. Since the seventeenth century the Opera has represented traditional high culture in Chinese performance art. The Beijing Opera is comprised of the elements of music, dance, combat, choreography and acrobatics. It is a highly-stylized art form: facial expressions and gestures serve a pantomime purpose—a visual vocabulary whose symbolism is understood by the audience. Realistic representations of plot and actions are not desirable and props are minimal. At our show the actors performed on a bare stage with a yellow curtain hanging behind them, rendering their elaborate costumes all the more striking. They wore stylized robes—red and blue with gold embroidery is code for characters of high rank, and yellow indicates the Imperial Family; other types of robes and colors are indicative of various stock characters. My group had the opportunity to watch the actors applying their theatrical make-up—the painting of highly formalized symbolic designs upon their faces. Apprenticeship from a young age is necessary for actors to master the established repertoire of facial expressions and gestures, vocal enunciations and pitches, along with the musical instruments and songs, martial arts and weaponry, and dance and acrobatics. The tour included a visit to a school that provides training in theater for select pupils. A group of students approximately eight years of age performed a concert for my group. They were lively and smiling, but very orderly, children.

The Chinese people showed off their artisanal specialties in manufactory tours. A silk factory provided demonstrations of the creation of hand-loomed rugs, and the guide informed the tour group that many young women lost their eyesight early in life as a result of the close work of the high thread-count weaves. A jade company demonstrated the production of jewelry and sculptures. Both tours concluded in the retail shopping areas of the establishments.

The Great Wall is one of the highlights of my trip to China. The Wall was begun in the seventh century B.C., and construction continued until the seventeenth century A.D. The entire length of the different portions of the Wall combined is approximately 13,000 miles. My tour group ascended the Wall at Badaling, a portion built in the early sixteenth century. Like a city wall, it is a pedestrian thoroughfare high up in the Juyongguan Pass. The Wall snakes and follows the mountainous terrain, conforming itself to the topography. The mountains are very high, grey rock. The highest aspects are bare; lower down there is green scrub. I scampered up and down the stone block walkway, steep steps interspersed with level portions, and crenelated stations at intervals. Where the ascent or descent are more taxing handrails have been added. Tourists were taking photographs of each other and looking at both Wall and mountains in wonder. The guide pointed to where we could see Tibet in the distance. From a vendor I purchased a laminated certificate with my photo on it that is printed "Memory of Climbing the Great Wall," "Not a lucky hero until one reaches the Great Wall," and "I have ascended the Badaling Great Wall."

There was one more prominent destination in the Beijing-area leg of the tour: the Sacred Way to the Ming Emperors' Tombs. In 1421 Emperor Yongle erected the first tomb on this site, and the next twelve emperors built their tombs here, too. The Sacred Way leads to the Changling Tomb of the Emperor Yongle and the

Empress Quian. From there it branches out to the sacred ways to the other sacred tombs. All thirteen tombs conform to the same layout of arches, gates, palaces and pavilions. Three of the tombs are open to visitors. The Sacred Way starts at the Memorial Arch, whose roof is made of round marble tiles with upturned corners, and continues to the Big Red Gate, which has a center door for the deceased and is flanked by two doors for everyone else. The Sacred Way is a wide stone-paved avenue lined on either side with trees and with stone sculptures. An outdoor Ming Dynasty museum, the Sacred Way contains statues of notable personages, horses, elephants, camels, and other animals. The Sacred Way then comes to the Ling 'en Palace, which resembles the structures of the Forbidden City in design and decoration—from the yellow tile roofs to the white marble balustrades on the three terraces. The Dingling Tomb built at the end of the sixteenth century has two rooms displaying the Ming Dynasty artifacts, ranging from gold coins to armor to the Empress's Phoenix Crown. The round, helmet-like crown is made of jade inlaid with jewels. Beneath the Tomb is a marble underground palace. The third tomb open to the public is the Zhaoling Tomb, which is an extensively-restored complex-museum showcasing a trove of Ming treasures.

From Beijing the tour group was ferried to Xian in a small plane. We were each given a plane ticket that had a name on it, but not our own names; the guide told us not to worry. In Xian we would be continuing our explorations of the cities of the dead, cities which had been constructed for an afterlife. Xian today is a modern metropolis characterized by its high-tech software and aerospace industries. Xian is a very old city, too—the remains of a village dating to 5000 B.C. were discovered here (Banpo). Qin Shi Huang Museum was our destination. It is often referred to as "the eighth wonder of the world," and is the tomb of the first Qin Emperor.

Discovered in the twentieth century by farmers digging a well, the tomb complex is a complete underground city. Soon after his accession to the throne, circa 200 B.C., the Emperor ordered the conscription of thousands of workers to build the palace in which he would reign in the next life. The city below the ground has three strata of underground water courses. Although the wooden walls of the underground city were burned in a peasant's uprising and an invasion, the underground relics have been preserved in a time capsule. The Emperor's copper coffin survives, as well as three thousand years of artifacts of bronze, silver, gold, and terra cotta. These include serving vessels, statuary, and realistic paintings.

The army is the primary enticement here. The underground city is defended by an army arranged in military formations four wide in corridors. Three archaeological excavation pits of about fifty-two acres contain about eight-thousand Terra Cotta Soldiers, some in pieces but many intact. Instead of moving them to a museum, the Chinese constructed a museum over the working archaeological dig. Visitors in the gallery surrounding the pits can watch archaeologists at work. A museum houses the funerary treasures of the Emperor in cases in other areas of the museum complex.

Inside Pit 1 is a large battle formation with vanguard, flank guards, chariots and infantry—fifty chariots and 6,000 soldiers. Each of the life-size soldiers is realistically sculpted, having its unique stance, face, dress, and expression. Individual hairs are visible in their topknots and braids. Their leather garments have grommets, tassels, tunics, and belts. Terra Cotta sleeves have natural folds, and the bottoms of the terra cotta shoes have traction. The harnesses and reins of the horses are formed of chains made of bracelet-like stone links. The soldiers, horses, chariots, and paraphernalia were at one time brightly painted, not the uniform shade of brown they are now. Pit 3 is a command center with a store of chariots and horses, weapons and deer horns (which were used in religious exercises prior to battle). Pit 2 is a less-excavated site containing infantry, archers, chariots and cavalry. It still contains remnants of burnt wooden structures. The array of weaponry is comprehensive for the army of the time, with bows, crossbows, halberds and spears, whose bronze is still sharp and is not rusted, protected by an ancient rust-inhibiting agent.

I spent that evening strolling the city streets. The brick-paved sidewalks are well-lit and tree-lined. The avenue is wide and there was a lot of traffic. The next morning I walked the Xian City Wall. Constructed soon after the Emperor's Tomb, the wall is about sixteen miles in length and about forty to fifty feet wide. Then my tour group was given the opportunity to visit a local family and look at their home. The husband and wife did not speak much beyond a greeting. Their house had a green tile roof with upward-curved corners. A spinning wheel sat in front of it. Exterior walls were brick. Interior walls were plaster with peeling paint. The floor was bare concrete. Simple floral curtains hung on the windows. A narrow bed and a chair were covered with sheets. A television sat on a desk, and a coffee table was pushed against a wall. Those were all the furnishings in the single room. A little grey-and-white kitten was observing our movements. One of the group asked the guide whether she was a pet or dinner, and the guide replied, "Chinese eat everything with legs but tables and everything with wings but planes."

The last evening in Xian my group feasted on a wonderful dinner in a restaurant which featured dumplings. My delicious vegetarian dumplings were served in a wicker steamer, and they were molded into the shapes of birds and other animals. After dinner we attended a Tang Dynasty Show, a spectacle featuring beautiful women clad in elegant silk gowns and elaborate coiffures dancing with scarves billowing as if they were fluid extensions of their arms. Musicians played traditional instruments whose names I do not know. Actors in robes of blue with gold with red embroidered sashes carried lettered boxes made of silk on poles above their heads. Although I did not understand all the symbolism involved, the beauty and pageantry were incredible.

From Xian the tour took me to Chongqing. It is a smog-filled city of grey concrete buildings cleft by a four-lane thoroughfare where we were. I walked the ghostly streets and saw a few pedestrians and a lot of soldiers and military vehicles. The streets had been cleared for the Pan-Asian Cities Conference that was to begin that day. In the evening I boarded the ship that would be taking me through the Three Gorges of the Yangtze River: the Victoria Queen.

The Victoria Queen has five decks above the waterline, all with balconies, and a top deck with lounge chairs. It would be home for the next three days. I had a comfortable cabin with two twin beds. On deck that night we were treated to a magnificent fireworks display on the river, a welcome for the Pan-Asian dignitaries arriving for the conference. The boat sailed the brown water of the Yangtze to the Qtang Gorge, a deep cut in the mountains through which the Yangtze River flows. As we sailed, the gorges became narrower and narrower, necessitating our transfer to smaller vessels—sampans. About twenty passengers in life vests sat in the small boats covered with thatched canopies. The guide took photos of the passengers wearing traditional Chinese straw hats that had charms hanging from the brims—the gorge in the background. We were among the last people to view the gorges before the river was flooded to raise the water level 100 feet, for which project more than a million people had to be forcibly relocated. The reason for the flooding had to do with the construction of the Three Gorges Dam, which was proposed to supply ten percent of all Chinese electricity, according to our guide (the majority of the Chinese population resides in the east). In the course of the river cruise we visited the Three Gorges Dam.

We ate meals on board and enjoyed entertainment—a fashion show of historical Chinese costume, Tai Chi and Mahjong instruction, and acupuncture demonstration upon a volunteer. When we reached the Shibaozhai Temple we were greeted by a Lion Dance. Animal masks are part of a long tradition among the various Chinese mythologies and are linked to a Buddhist tale of a lion who helped people drive away evil spirits. Our lion was of the Northern Lion type—with a red mane and a yellow body. Two acrobats create the lion's movements as he dances to the music provided by the musicians who accompany him. The lion dances to bring happiness to those he visits.

The nineteenth-century twelve-story pavilion below the temple was constructed to facilitate climbing the hill to the temple. The pavilion is built leaning into the hill. Narrow ladder-like stairs lead from one level to the next. At various levels cultural artifacts are displayed and sellers purvey goods from umbrella-covered stalls. The temple has green tile curved roofs, one upon the other, the corners adorned with elegantly carved open-mouthed dragons. The doorway is heavily carved and elaborately decorated in yellow-painted inset panels. The Yangtze having been flooded since I was there, Shibaozhai now sits on a lake, and the hill is an island in the river.

The tour concluded in Shanghai, where I remained two more days on my own. The city's modern architecture has achieved astounding feats. The skyline is quite distinctive. I indulged in some designer shopping: I purchased a Moschino t-shirt featuring a *Moulin Rouge* motif in a Chinese city—how's that for cosmopolitan! I found a Starbucks—which had coffee and bread *in the afternoon!* And I visited Old Shanghai, a city of traditional Chinese buildings with sliding doors and upturned green tile roofs; I explored some of them. I was enchanted by the Yu Yuan Garden, a grotto of rocks and greenery in an enclosed courtyard. A covered footbridge reaches over the water. Over the marble balustrade I could see the goldfish swimming in the pond. I bade farewell there to China—China of the bustling modern cities and of their macabre counterparts in the extensive array of subterranean metropolises built for the dead to live in the second time around.

TRAVELING IN THE BRAVE NEW WORLD

Orwell Was Off by Thirty-Six Years
or, 2020 is the New *1984*

We three friends had planned this trip for months—a lark, a ghost hunt, a witch hunt. I was to stay at the landmark Seelbach hotel in Louisville, Kentucky. My California writer friend was to join me there for a tour of the haunted hotel, and then we were to make a pleasurable jaunt through the attractions of Bluegrass country. We were to end our trip by meeting up with our North Carolinian writer friend in Adams, Tennessee, to search for the relics of the infamous Bell Witch.

Daily our plans became more and more tentative. First there was a pandemic of the new coronavirus—a souped-up cold bug that moved extra-quickly from person to person and had a high mortality rate, compared to the usual annual death toll from influenza. The government agencies issued guidelines for protecting one's health.

Then the "guidelines" became "rules." America itself was placed under house arrest—they called it "quarantine." *The language itself was becoming more and more Orwellian Doublespeak*. Furthermore, people no longer had the right to decide how they would care for their own health.

I was an "essential worker," which meant I was under house arrest with work privileges. I was given papers to prove that I was essential. That meant that, unlike non-essential people who were now losing their jobs, I could go not only to the grocery store, but I could go to work as well. Having these "papers" made me feel as if I were living in East Berlin or a Communist bloc nation. I looked all about me for a Resistance movement to join. All that I want to live for is embodied in the Bill of Rights and the Constitution of the United States of America—and these rights were now null and void. The government said we need only give up our freedom: the government would take care of us.

My L.A. friend was not essential. She suffered social and mental deprivation under months of house arrest, during which time her only human contact was "virtual." Driven to her limit, she faced the ultimate choices—suicide or flight. Made of strong stuff, she chose the latter and fled California. She has become a refugee, a nomad, until her home becomes free again. Being forced to work from home, my Carolinian friend suffered the loss of personal interaction with his students; he was kept busy, but he felt his work was less effective and less fulfilling.

Having seized unprecedented power during what they termed a "national emergency," the government followed the usual and customary practices of kidnappers. To brainwash their victims, kidnappers (as well as sex slavers and cult leaders) begin by isolating their victims—and then they destroy their self-esteem. In America, proud working people were forced to stand six feet apart in food lines. After the salons were closed and the stores ran out of Clairol, women could no longer pretend that their hair color was natural, and they were made to swallow their pride. People in pain had to put off "nonessential" orthopedic surgeries and cancer treatments.

After a few months, the government began to gradually restore these "nonessential" things—all the while saying that they might need to lock us down again—for our own good. This is the way kidnappers engender dependence, gratitude—and even love—in their victims: they take what their victims have by force, and they return some of their plunder with benevolence, so that the victim is grateful to them.

I became aware that I had become a subject in a massive psycho-social experiment of Cyclopean proportions—like a lab rat in a plexiglass box with levers to push for rewards or electric shocks.

The variable at stake was the extent to which people could be compelled to live life *virtually*, rather than *really*. People were instructed to attend virtual classes, concerts, and funerals instead of real. "Social Distancing" became the new soma. Life was remodeled into lone individuals talking to glowing screens in the isolation of social distancing, rather than interacting with physical, sweaty, smelly, perfumed, warm, flesh-and-blood people—people who look here and there when speaking with you, rather than gazing directly at you (or at a screen or webcam); and people who react according to the temperature of the room, and the weather, and noises surrounding them, rather than speaking in seclusion.

All interactions were supposed to occur on fiber optic cables, monitored by Big Brother, the puppeteer from whom all communication flowed and to whom it returned. Communications were being monitored for "virus tracking" (and no one need fear a violation of his privacy, Big Brother reassured us). We were told that to question Big Brother was to put our neighbors at risk. And our neighbors were encouraged to turn us in if we were not obedient.

We could take no more. We packed our bags. We traveled, *this time*, to salvage our dignity as human individuals, and our right to self-determination. To live our lives. To live the Bill of Rights. We were determined to take our little vacation—what might be left of it—with all the lockdowns and cowering public. To live as free people.

Four days before I was to leave for Louisville, violent protests erupted in that city—and in cities across America. The immediate cause was the alleged murder of a citizen by a policeman. Over the last few years, there have been many such cases of police brutality in the news, and racial tensions have been simmering and have blown the lid off the pot several times, culminating in violent activities, such as which were happening now. Oppressed people can take it only so long.

This latest incident that sparked riots nationwide occurred within the larger framework of a general oppression of the nation: for months innocent citizens had been locked down en masse in their own homes—effectively under house arrest—because of the virus. Gun sales had soared in the immediate aftermath of the lockdown announcement, and store shelves were emptied of ammunition. Never before had people feared the U.S. government as much. People were at their wits' end, trying to hold it together emotionally and financially: as the bills began to mount they were being deprived of the means of earning a livelihood. Many were evicted from their homes. Tensions in the once-free country were already dangerously high. The government had just begun to gradually restore some freedoms—to prevent wholesale revolt, to release a little steam—when the death of a black man in police custody caused an explosion of the human will to live free.

Those conducting this socio-psychological experiment will learn from their mistakes. The next time they will be able to maintain a tighter control—and a longer. Make no mistake, this is only a first run, a rehearsal. Someone means to wean people away from other people, and *to give them computers in their place*. Ultimately, they intend that people will bond only with their computers, and the computers will lead to Big Brother.

We determined to stay our course. This was to be a different kind of vacation, it seemed. A grim adventure. We were fighting for our lives.

The Bell Witch Project

This was our Plague Year. We took flight—flight from the despotism that was poisoning American life. Once-free people were being forced to stay in their homes. Many were deprived of their livelihoods. The Bill of Rights was suspended. America was under house arrest. We three friends had long planned this trip, and we kept our rendezvous. We convened in Adams, Tennessee to search for the Bell Witch.

I arrived in Louisville on the Monday following a weekend of rioting in that city. In Minneapolis, a black man had died in police custody, and the officer was charged with murder. In response, protests and riots had been occurring in cities all across America.

The landmark Seelbach Hotel, where I—and only five other people—were staying, was boarded up and secured. Two of the hotel windows had been broken over the weekend, and now they were all boarded up on ground level to protect them from rioters. The staff were nervous.

The city streets were empty. I walked by empty parking lots and plywood-covered buildings. Many windows had been broken. Glass was all over the sidewalk in front of the windows of the drugstore across the street from the Seelbach, where some crushed glass still clung to the frames. Homeless people were the only ones in sight—except for the numerous carpenters pounding their hammers to put up plywood on the doors and windows of buildings up and down the city blocks, and except for the people from window replacement companies who were assessing the damage. Paint and signs on windows read, "Black Lives Matter,"

"Say Her Name," "Black-owned Business," and "Small Family Owned, Muslim Business."

All but two of the restaurants on the riverfront streets were closed. A hotel employee told me that Dunkin Donuts had been looted. I ate a delicious Mexican meal at a restaurant near the Seelbach, but when I inquired about desserts at 3:40 PM, the waiter told me I had to leave. They were closing up and boarding up the storefront. Carpenters were already at work. They were nervous; they wanted to be finished before the protesters returned.

Businesses had just been opening that week—after months of having been forcibly closed down because of the pandemic. Many would never open again.

I am a walker, and so I walked about with my camera taking pictures of the surreal scenes of a usually busy tourist area that was boarded up in this first week of June, of the empty streets of Louisville, and of the shattered windows. Louisville was a ghost town. One recurring mental image my mind kept replaying was that of a group of storytelling friends—the ones who had fled the Plague in the *Decameron*. I pictured the people of Ireland, too, who suffered in the cholera epidemic (as described by Dacre Stoker in his memorable lecture at *StokerCon*), and I kept envisioning the bodies that were piling up in the empty streets of Dublin whilst people hid in their homes. The movie that kept asserting itself into my consciousness was *The Last Man on Earth*: I had numerous flashbacks of Vincent Price, scavenging on empty streets, as I sought an open restaurant where I could get some dinner. I knew that I had to get back to the hotel well before dark, before the protesters came out, in case there was violence again—and I felt that, like Vincent, I was waiting for the vampires to come out of their warrens. I knew I might be sorry if I lingered too late outside. I watched carefully as protesters, wearing anti-virus masks and carrying signs, began to arrive in twos and threes. I re-entered my beautiful hotel and began taking photos inside.

The next day my friend Amanda from California joined me at

the Seelbach for a tour of the historic hotel. A beautiful Beaux-Arts building in its own right, I had selected this hotel because of its other outstanding qualities: first, it was haunted; and, second, it had been renovated in the 1980s by *Dark Shadows* star Roger Davis. FDR and JFK had slept here. Also F. Scott Fitzgerald and Al Capone. Its heyday was the Prohibition era.

Gracious is the most suitable word for the personal attentions I received during my residence at the Seelbach. Seelbach employee Christiane provided my friend and myself a tour that was heavily laced with anecdotes from the hotel's history. She showed us the marble lobby surrounded by murals that tell stories from the history of Kentucky, and the skylight above with eight hundred panes of glass. These had both been covered over during previous "modernisations" of the hotel. She told us that Roger Davis had had the murals restored and the skylight revealed. She took our photo on what she called "the most photographed staircase in the world," a Y-shaped staircase with ornate brass rails that joins the lobby and the mezzanine. We climbed the stairs to the ornate Oak Room, a one-time gentlemen's billiard room, later a restaurant. It was now poised for a renovation, Christiane told us, which had been put on hold because of the pandemic.

Then she took us into a small room off of the Oak Room. It was also paneled in heavily-molded oak wood. A round table and four chairs were in the center. Christiane said that Al Capone had run an illegal casino there. He was purported to have sat at the table, facing the mirror so that he could see his opponent's cards. She drew our attention to a sealed door which blended seamlessly into the oak panels of the walls. It used to lead to tunnels below the city that opened onto the bank of the Ohio River, and it had served as an escape route and a conduit for illegally transported alcoholic beverages.

Christiane told us of the Blue Lady, the ghost of a guest who had died in 1936 by falling down the elevator shaft after hearing that her husband was dead. She showed us the breathtaking

Grand Ballroom, which is often used for wedding receptions. In *The Great Gatsby*, F. Scott Fitzgerald set the Buchanan wedding in the ballroom of the Seelbach, where he could be found so much of the time.

Fitzgerald would usually frequent the nightclub which was in the Rathskeller at the Seelbach. A one-of-a-kind Rookwood Pottery Room, it is a vast subterranean chamber of burnt-orange and sage green-tiled walls and floors. These are surmounted by a painted leather, medieval-style vaulted ceiling held up by myriad columns. Columns, walls, and floors are made of Rookwood Pottery (which was once made in Cincinnati). This is a magical space which conjures images of the Brothers Grimm story of *The Twelve Dancing Princesses*, whirling out of control in a ballroom. Rookwood pelicans—a German symbol of good luck—surround the myriad columns and look at you from all sides of the room.

After the tour, Amanda and I walked to the Ohio River and the deserted riverwalk. We enjoyed the peaceful beauty of the sun reflected by the water, and we marveled that we could see Indiana on the far bank of the river. We took pictures of the paddleboats—sadly not running—casualties of the pandemic and the riots. Then we headed out of the city center to the Whitehall House and Gardens. Although the house was closed to tours because of the pandemic, the grounds were still open. We clambered up onto the porch and peeked in the windows of the white Greek Revival mansion. Behind its two-story pillars, capped by a triangular cornice, is a cool, shaded porch, which we found refreshing in the summer heat. As we relaxed in the rocking chairs, we observed a bird in his nest at the top of a pillar. We strolled among the succulent, green plants and brightly-colored flowers of the formal Florentine garden, which is home to numerous rabbits.

It was getting to the dinner hour, a little later, even. Louisville was subject to a curfew. Amanda returned to her hotel, and I to the Seelbach. I searched for a restaurant; I found a pizzeria. It was the only place open, and business was brisk. Many customers came in to pick up their orders as I waited, and each one greeted me and said, "Keep Safe." The owner told me that over the weekend his neighbor (the owner of a restaurant with a sign on the window that read "Small Family Business, Muslim") saved the pizzeria by appealing to the protesters. As I carried my pizza to the hotel I observed the arrival of protesters with black masks and signs; they arrived in small groups and headed down the street toward the river, then vanished around the corner. I sat on the hotel steps to eat. Helicopters were circling overhead. Business owners were pounding nails into the plywood they were putting up over their doors and windows. The Seelbach is situated at an intersection, where soon I witnessed a crowd of protesters congregating. Cars blocked the sides of the intersection, and a person with a bullhorn stood in the center and talked (I couldn't make out the words). I walked there and took photos of the peaceful protest, about a fifty-fifty mix of black and white citizens. After ten minutes or so, the cars were moved from the intersection and the protesters moved down the street.

Inside the Seelbach, the employees were worried about our safety. I shared some wine and watched the television coverage of the protests and political responses with another guest, who was in Louisville for work. When I went to bed I waited for the Blue Lady. During the night I opened my eyes and saw the ambient street light coming through the sheer curtains, creating a very lovely, ghostly vision.

When I awakened the next morning, I had, alas, seen no Blue Lady. I walked at sunrise. I took pictures of the great baseball bat that leans against the Slugger Museum—the bat is taller than that five-story museum structure. I found another giant-sized piece of art: a 120-foot gilt reproduction of Michelangelo's David. The juxtaposition of the two sculptures is somewhat jarring—but jarring can be kind of cool. My walk took me to the Galt House at the River, where I found that a snack bar was open inside the vast and empty hotel. The menu was reduced to only a few selections—supplies were scarce. I enjoyed my coffee looking out the large picture windows at the Ohio River. Then I left to join Amanda for an excursion to Bowling Green.

Bowling Green, Kentucky is home to the *Lost River Cave*. Our North Carolina friend Michael joined us here. The hospitable guide beckoned to us to follow him along the woodland path, past the zip lines and the butterfly sanctuary, to the blue holes. The blue holes are places where the water of the underground river comes to the surface. They are a frosted marine blue color; the guide told us the color is caused by the calcium oxide in the river. He said the placid-looking water runs swiftly beneath the surface, reaching the Gulf of Mexico in just three weeks from where we stood.

We approached the entrance to the cave. We were issued seat cushions that would double as flotation devices in the event of a person overboard. We entered a small boat that rocked menacingly as I inched down the length of it to let the others aboard. The Lost River Cave Boat Tour is a fascinating journey into a mountain crevice. We had to bend over from the waist initially—the ceiling of the cave is very low. Having sailed passed that point, we could then sit upright. It was dark in the cave; I recall only one aperture allowing in natural light from above. The guide shone his lantern on the cave walls and ceilings surrounding us, and on the water of the river, as he navigated through the shallow water. He talked of stalactites and stalagmites, mineral deposits, a room with Civil War graffiti, and one with Native American artifacts. He told us that there are legends of Jesse James hiding out in the cave. At one time the cave was used as a nightclub, he said. I had a hard time following his words: I was entranced by the cave itself. It is other-worldly, different from the other caves I have explored in Ohio and Virginia, because it is also a subterranean river.

After our spelunking experience we went into the historical center of Bowling Green, where we crossed Fountain Square Park in search of lunch. We observed a group of a few score protesters walking down the street toward the town center; among them were nearly a dozen policemen. The group appeared relaxed and friendly as they walked together. Following lunch, our Carolinian friend returned to Tennessee, where he was visiting family; and we returned to Louisville. We had a date with a ghost hunter, for a ghost walk.

Robert Parker, of *Louisville Ghost Walks*, met us at the Seelbach Hotel. We had rescheduled the ghost walk for an earlier hour to make sure we finished our tour before the curfew—and before the protesters returned to the streets. He escorted us down Fourth Street to the Brown Hotel. It was boarded up and empty of guests. A manager was stationed at a kiosk in the entranceway. He greeted us ghost hunters and cordially welcomed us inside. Robert began to tell us stories about J. Graham Brown, who built the hotel in 1923 and who still makes appearances with his dog Woozum. Mr. Brown still stands at the balcony outside his office to look down upon the opulent lobby below; a smell of cigars or a rush of cold air tells that he is nearby. Numerous hotel employees and guests have reported seeing him, as well as our guide, Robert. Robert also told us of an evil presence in Room 615, who pulled on his arm and bit a lady's shoulder. Pieces on a chess set in the mezzanine have moved themselves. The hotel manager added a number of ghostly anecdotes to Robert's collection, and he gave us a private tour of the magnificent establishment. Its plush and beautiful soft rose and green carpeting was made in England. The restaurant and seating areas in the lobby are a decorative arts treasure trove.

When we exited the building we observed military vehicles pulling into the parking lot across the street. They were filled with armed National Guardsmen in camouflage and riot gear, wearing face shields and canteens hanging from their uniforms.

We walked down the boarded-up street to the old Key Theater, which is now a restaurant, where a scent of perfume, the sound of footsteps, and self-opening and closing doors attest to the presence of spirits. Then we stopped outside the Palace, a ninety-year old theater that closed in the 1970s, where the first talkies were shown.

The projectionist Barney died there, and he is currently playing pranks with lights and doors and touching people. A woman with no face has been seen on the stairs, and children in the window. We visited the Mercury Theater, which had an illegal casino and its own tunnel entrances in the time of the Prohibition, and now has its ghosts. We stopped at the Body Shop, a striptease club that has a ghost upstairs which appears in mirrors, ransacks dressing rooms, and locks people in their rooms; Robert says they don't even use the top two floors any more. It turns out that the Mexican restaurant I enjoyed on my first day in Louisville has a haunted basement; the owners cannot communicate with the ghost, Robert says, because of a language barrier. We ended up back at the Seelbach, where Robert told us of the Lady in Blue—and the ghost of a man with white hair and a red necktie (most likely a brother of Louis and Otto Seelbach, who built the hotel); he has seen the ghost himself. My friend and I parted ways, to get a good night's repose in preparation for witch-hunting in Tennessee the next day.

The Bell Witch is the oldest continuous American ghost story; and she is the first ghost accused of killing her victim in this country. There are conflicting opinions regarding whether she is a poltergeist, a witch, or a demon. To learn more of her story is the reason for this trip. Amanda joined me in the morning for a drive to Adams, Tennessee, population less than a thousand. Adams is situated on the Red River, a tributary of the Cumberland. It was still wilderness when the Bell family moved there. By the 1820s Robertson County was known for its tobacco plantations and thoroughbred horses. We drove five hours over country roads—we kept getting lost and driving in circles, because many of the roads are not marked—to get to Adams. When we stopped for gas I noticed a pentacle around the cashier's neck. I asked the woman whether she was a practitioner or just interested, and she said she was a practitioner. I was delighted to meet a Kentucky witch on the way to find a Tennessee witch.

From 1817 to 1821 the Bell family was terrorized by the entity known as The Bell Witch. Betsy, the youngest daughter, was subjected to blows and punches; her blankets were removed from her bed as she slept. John Sr., the father, was poisoned by the witch, after having endured a long and debilitating illness that was characterized by difficulty swallowing. The whole family were harassed. It all began with sightings of a doglike creature and a big bird; then they heard gnawing at the beds and chains rattling. By the time it was all over, the Bell Witch had had lengthy conversations with the Bells and their friends and neighbors—even Andrew Jackson, who was passing through Adams.

Ever since that time there have been debates over how much of the story is hoax, and how much is history. In preparation for my investigation, I read *Our Family Trouble: The Story of the Bell Witch of Tennessee* by Richard Williams Bell, a manuscript written circa 1846 and published in 1894 by Martin Van Buren Ingram. James Allen Bell, grandson to John Bell, Senior, released his father's manuscript to the publisher after everyone who had had anything to do with the events had died; therefore, there was no living person to verify the facts at the time of publication. There is no original draft in Richard Williams Bell's handwriting. Reading the book one learns that the witch hated the smell of the slaves and presented multiple autobiographies when asked who she was. I also watched two movies: *The Bell Witch Haunting* (2013) in which a modern family moves onto the Bell property; and *An American Haunting* (2005), which presents the theory that the witch was Kate Batts, a business adversary of John Bell, Sr.

We rendezvoused with Michael in Adams. The Bell Witch Cave was our first stop—the purported lair of the witch. It was not open. While we attempted to find someone who could let us in, multiple vehicles from several states pulled into the drive. Having driven this far into the countryside to learn about the witch, we were all of us disappointed.

We went next to the Bellwood Cemetery on Highway 41, where many of the Bells are resting. In a marble-enclosed space for the graves of Bell family members (other prominent citizens can be buried outside the enclosed space), there is a monument. The monument tells the Bell Family lineage; it begins, "John Bell 1750–1820 and his wife Lucy Williams, Pioneer Settlers from Halifax & Edgecombe Co., N.C." and then enumerates the names of their children and grandchildren. We thought that this was going to be all that we would be able to see of the Bell Witch history—until we spoke with the caretaker, who was cutting the grass. Himself an expert on the Bell Witch legend, he shared some information with us and then advised us to talk to Tim at the restaurant.

Next to the cemetery is the old school building—which is now subdivided into a restaurant, antique mall, museum and Adams archives. Here we sat down to order lunch, and we asked the hostess if we could speak with Tim. She said that he was not there, but she would call him. She did. He came right over with his hand-whittled walking stick; he makes them with his penknife and sells them. Turns out Tim Henson is a local guy with a master's degree in history, who has become the official historian of Adams and of The Bell Witch. He has worked with "Hollywood" quite a bit, it turns out—on *Arts & Entertainment* and various other television documentaries. He is eager to share his knowledge with anyone interested.

He told us the Bell family left North Carolina in a wagon train in 1804. It was a period of evil omens. In 1810 there was a comet. The New Madrid Earthquakes in Missouri (1811–1812) shook Adams—the shocks were large enough to cause the Mississippi River to run backwards. In 1815 an Indonesian volcano spewed forth enough ash to darken the sky throughout 1816, and in Adams corn failed and cattle died for lack of sunlight. He told us that the Red River Church of Christ is the repository of most of the records relating to John Bell, Sr.—including the lawsuit over the failed sale of a slave girl to Kate Batts which resulted in John's excommunication from the church (in *An American Haunting* John Bells's crime is usury). Kate Batts regularly offended people by coming to church late, her three slaves in tow—enough reason for people to think her a witch at the time.

Tim described the conditions in Robertson County at the beginning of the nineteenth century: there was no running water or electricity; people subsisted in poverty; and superstition, infections, and yellow fever were rampant. A Dr. Bell had wanted to write the story, Tim said, but the family was opposed to the idea. The family did give their consent to Ingram's presentation of the manuscript, though. Tim Henson thinks that the lack of primary information suggests a cover-up of some kind. He said he thought the family had been ashamed of the skeleton in their closet; *The Blair Witch Project* rekindled interest in the Bell Witch story, he told us. In the museum, we watched a documentary and saw an original 1894 edition of the Ingram book. Then Tim showed us around Adams.

Tim is a prominent citizen in Adams, and thus he was able to escort us onto private property to see Kate Batts's land, which had adjoined the Bell stake. He showed us where the well had been located on her property. He guided us through farms and forest, telling us intriguing tales of the Bell clan. He pointed out the creek where Andrew Jackson had met The Bell Witch and had enjoyed sparring with her. He took us into a cornfield where the worn stones (some only fragments) of the John Bell, Jr. family graves can be found; some of the stones had been stolen, he said. The land had been recently plowed, and Tim told us he likes to search for arrowheads and other historical artifacts in newly turned earth, and so we all looked with him for a while.

He took us next into the woods which had grown up over John Bell, Sr.'s grave (its headstone had been replaced in 1957, after the original had been stolen) and the graves of some of his slaves, which are marked by pieces of flat rock among the foliage. He took us to an ancient well that is on the Bell family property. He brought us back to the museum—to which an original log cabin of the Bell family had been moved in 1982. The first Bell home had been built in 1810 and taken down at a later date, and usable materials would have been salvaged for use in the new house. This cabin had been on the Bell estate and lived in by Bells.

Adams hosts an annual Bell Witch Fall Festival and presents *Spirit*, a dramatization of the Bell Witch legend by local playwright David Alford. They also present *Smoke*, another drama by Alford, which tells the story of the Night Riders and the Tobacco Wars of Middle Tennessee.

Reluctantly, we had to leave—we had to be back in Louisville before the curfew. Tim warned us not to take anything like the rocks which people were always sending back—they usually experienced bad luck when they took Bell Witch mementos home with them. We bade goodbye to Tim, and to Michael, who was to return to his family in Tennessee. Amanda & I returned to Louisville, to go our own separate ways in the morning. My graveyard dirt was securely packed in my luggage

APPENDIX

Creepy Cat's Guide to Entertaining

Whether one is an armchair traveler or is infected with the wanderlust, she will occasionally wish to enjoy the pleasures of darkness within her own home. Several festive seasons lend themselves to macabre celebrations and entertaining at home: the summer and winter solstices, All Hallows Eve, Walpurgis Night, and Creepy Cat's favorite St. George's Eve. Creepy Cat offers her suggestions for an evening of creeping out one's friends:

St. George's Eve is the night preceding St. George's Day. St. George's Day is May 6 in the Gregorian calendar, although some do prefer to reference the old Julian calendar date of April 23. St. George is traditionally portrayed as a knight on horseback slaying a dragon, symbol of the forces of evil; St. George's Eve, however, is when the evil spirits are out in force:

It is the eve of St. George's Day. Do you not know that tonight when the clock strikes midnight, all the evil things in the world will have full sway?

The villagers warn Jonathan Harker as he embarks for Dracula's castle, in Bram Stoker's *Dracula*, and they beg him to wait until the next day to go. This duality of spring holidays is the equivalent of the autumn pairing of All Hallows Eve and the following day, All Saints Day (St. George's Eve and Halloween are "Fat Tuesdays," of a sort, for the Evil Things on the nights before the religious feast days of St. George and All the Saints).

The ancient traditions of European agrarian societies evolved from people's various efforts to defend themselves against malevolent spirits and other evil entities on such dangerous nights. Halloween defensive traditions include Jack-o-lanterns and bonfires. Other protective measures include burying milk to protect the cattle from witches; wearing one's shirt turned inside-out; sleeping with a knife under the pillow; wearing a hat to prevent a witch from slipping a bridle over one's head; and placing garlic on doors and windows.

Today St. George's Eve is a spring Halloween. The Goth set, especially, honor the holiday, and many Goth weddings are performed on this day. Festivities based on *Dracula* are held annually in Whitby, England, where the *Demeter* came ashore, bringing Dracula to England. Should the reader feel inclined to treat his friends to a macabre soiree, Creepy Cat has suggestions. The reader most likely will find many additional horrific ideas in the corridors of her own sinister imagination.

Creating a dark frame of mind begins even before the guests arrive. Invitations should include the relevant quotation from *Dracula* about St. George's Eve and a brief explanation of the holiday. Creepy Cat encouraged a guest at one of her bashes to memorize (*before the party*) the Gypsy Maleva's lines from Universal's *The Wolf Man*:

> *Even a man who is pure in heart*
> *and says his prayers by night*
> *may become a wolf when the wolfbane blooms*
> *and the autumn moon is bright.*

The guest was warned to keep her performance a secret. A second guest was instructed to draw a pentagram on her palm, but not to tell the others. At the party, Creepy Cat provided the *gypsy* with a fringed shawl and a crystal ball and cued her to "read" the other guest's palm while reciting her lines. Both guests were surprised, as were everyone else, and the performance was a great hit.

Creepy Cat decorates her front porch with a black wreath and hangs garlic on the door. Inside the house black and red candles are everywhere, tapers and columns. Creepy Cat puts to good use the paraphernalia she has collected on her annual holidays in Salem—little black cauldrons, witches' brooms, human-shaped candles, voodoo poppets—in tasteful arrangements. Her Halloween and macabre-themed Barbie dolls serve as centerpieces at her St. George's Eve socials.

As guests arrive at the door, Creepy Cat suggests the host gravely intones (with a Transylvanian accent, if she is able) Count Dracula's words of welcome to Jonathan Harker:

> *I bid you welcome to my house. Come freely. Go safely; and*
> *leave something of the happiness you bring.*

On the threshold the host should present each guest with a gothic-style ornate mirror and demand that the guest prove that he can cast a reflection. Creepy Cat guides each guest to a table upon which a black, embossed *Book of Shadows* (available where Wicca and goth articles are sold) is arranged with black and red taper candles; she asks guests to sign their names in red ink (betokening blood), as traditionally those accused of practicing the Dark Arts have been said to have signed the devil's book with their blood (N.B. *This* book is simply a guest list, for Creepy Cat's purpose is to laugh at evil things, not to condone them).

The host should encourage guests to explore their inner darkness by providing a suggested dress code of black, black, and more black. A crystal candy dish filled with *Kat Von D* lipsticks in shades of black and deep burgundy enhances the vampish mood and makes for a creepy fashion statement, as well as a fiendish party favor.

After everyone has been served beverages, including lavender-flavored water (lavender invokes the spirits) and been seated, the gypsy performance can begin. After the palm reading, guests can take their turns scrying in the crystal ball themselves; your guests will most likely be very creative.

Creepy Cat has a life-sized gauze-wrapped mummy who comes out for special occasions. Mummy stands guard over a table laden with prizes: tarot cards, incense, books on witchcraft and surviving the zombie apocalypse, vampire fangs, and t-shirts. Guests answering trivia questions win selections from the table. Here are some sample questions:

Define "widdershins:"

> *A Scottish dialect term for counterclockwise movement. In traditional lore from most of Europe, moving around something in a widdershins direction was unlucky, and could be used deliberately to curse someone. (Greer 518).*

And "breast divination:"

> *Reading a woman's personality by the shape of her breasts (Greer 72).*

These quotes are from *The New Encyclopedia of the Occult* by John Michael Greer (Llewellyn 2015), a useful source of information which Creepy Cat discovered in a picturesque little store in Salem. Guests who volunteer to read a selection from the book may take a prize. Other prizes will be awarded to winners of the card games that are next on the program—a deck of horror trivia questions and one of scary movie trivia. Creepy Cat likes VHS tapes for the convenience of stopping them at the scenes she wishes to play: Creepy Cat plays clips of the witches' scene around the cauldron in *Macbeth*, from Lugosi's *Dracula*, *The Wolf Man*, and *The Creature from the Black Lagoon* and awards prizes to the first person to name the movies correctly.

Following the competition for prizes, Creepy Cat invites her guests to take seats at various stations where games have been set up—tarot, board games (Creepy Cat adores the *Dark Shadows* game in which players construct a skeleton by pulling bones from a casket and hanging them on a scaffold), Ouija, oracle cards, and pinning the poppets—and the guests rotate among the various stations. Creepy Cat held an Exorcism at one of her famous soirees: Barbie, unfortunately, had been possessed by a devil—her head was turned backward! Creepy Cat erected a stake to which she tied Barbie, and she piled kindling at her little feet, to save her soul by burning her body, as was done in the olden days. Creepy Cat, however, thought of another way to come to Barbie's assistance: in the company of her St. George's Eve guests Creepy Cat performed an exorcism over the doll (she found the Rite of Exorcism of the Catholic Church in Montague Summers's *The History of Witchcraft and Demonology)* —and saved her from the devil! Now there was no need to roast the old girl; she looks so cute, however, tied to the stake, that Creepy Cat hasn't the heart to release her. To this day Barbie at the Stake remains on a shelf in Creepy Cat's library.

By this time the guests will want to relax. Creepy Cat makes them comfortable in front of the television to watch Bela Lugosi's *Dracula*. But first she gives them each a packet of lavender seeds so that they can grow gardens that will attract the spirits to their own homes. And then she gives them each a bottle of garlic tablets to protect them on the way home; just in case the garlic is inadequate, though, Creepy Cat provides each guest with a bandage large enough to cover two neck punctures and prevent the wounds from becoming infected.

Creepy Cat hopes that her reader shall derive both instruction and amusement from her guide for entertaining. She wishes that each of us should keep the macabre spirit alive in our hearts every day of the year.

Acknowledgements

Creepy Cat wishes to acknowledge the kind assistance and support of the very good friends without whom her book would never have been published.

With gratitude, she recognizes Scott Howarth, Information Technology Librarian, and the rest of the great staff at the public library of Perry, Ohio, on the shores of beautiful Lake Erie: they have provided invaluable midwifery services with the technical aspects of preparing her manuscript.

With heartfelt thanks and purrs, Creepy Cat also acknowledges authors Amanda Trujillo and Dr. Michael Potts, Professor of Philosophy at Methodist University, as well as lifelong friend Joyce Nelson, who have served as the principal readers and commentators—and godparents—to her literary progeny.

Also Available From

WORDCRAFTS PRESS

Before History Dies
by Jacob M. Carter

House of Madness
by Sara Harris

Devil's Charm
by Leslie Conner

Ill Gotten Gain
by Ralph E. Jarrells

Obedience
by Michael Potts

CPSIA information can be obtained
at www.ICGtesting.com
Printed in the USA
LVHW112045020921
696838LV00004B/13/J